Crest of the Diocese of Fort Wayne-South Bend,
in the window of the Archbishop's home

Archbishop Noll's official seal, showing
coat of arms detail

THE EXTRAORDINARY LIFE &
LEGACY OF ARCHBISHOP NOLL

CHAMPION
OF THE CHURCH

ANN BALL
WITH FATHER LEON HUTTON

Our Sunday Visitor Publishing Division
Our Sunday Visitor, Inc.
200 Noll Plaza
Huntington, IN 46750

ISBN-13: 978-1-59276-149-4
ISBN-10: 1-59276-149-6 (Inventory No. T200)
LCCN: 2005937558

Cover design by Monica Haneline
Cover photo courtesy of Our Sunday Visitor archives
Interior design by Sherri L. Hoffman
Interior photos used with permission

PRINTED IN THE UNITED STATES OF AMERICA

Contents

Dedication

No other prelate has had a greater impact or more lasting influence on the Catholic Church in America than Archbishop John Francis Noll. His ideas turned into action, which flowed into reality. His works live on, continuing to explain the truth and bring the beauty of the Catholic Faith to millions of Americans. His spirit lives on in Our Sunday Visitor and in those who strive to educate in defense of the Church and Christian values in society.

Although as Archbishop, he held an important and dignified position among the clergy, to those who knew and loved him he remained simply "the Bish," a good shepherd of his flock.

He was a "harmonizer" among the people. Warm, witty, and personable, he always addressed the many readers of his weekly newspaper in a loving and informal manner as "Friends of Our Sunday Visitor." A man ahead of his time, long before Vatican II John Noll understood, appreciated, and encouraged the work of the laity in Catholic action. A peacemaker at heart, without in any way compromising his high standards or the tenets of the Catholic faith, he brought the country to the realization that it was possible to be both Catholic and American.

This sketch of his life is dedicated to his beloved laity and the friends of Our Sunday Visitor.

Foreword

Scripture tells us, "By their fruits you shall know them." Archbishop John F. Noll was among the most fruitful of America's great bishops, and we at Our Sunday Visitor continue to reap the rich harvest of his legacy.

Yet the most enduring of his prodigious efforts — all accomplished while he was a full-time pastor and bishop — may not be the specific products that he created, but the passion and the energy with which he engaged American society, and the encouragement he gave to others to do the same.

Archbishop Noll was what is now known as "an early adopter." He embraced the communication tools of his day — print, radio, and television — with an eye toward how they could best serve the mission of the Church. He was also ahead of his time in understanding the vital role that laypeople could play in the life of the Church and in society. He encouraged lay involvement, believing that only through an educated and energetic laity could the Church hope to spread the Gospel and renew the nation.

He has not been the only bishop to found a newspaper, write books, and play a leadership role in the world beyond his diocese. But the lasting vitality of Archbishop Noll's legacy is unique.

The same newspaper he founded to defend the Church and teach the faithful continues to do so today. *The Priest* magazine today serves a clergy more embattled than ever before, but no less dedicated to their vocation. And many new publications have joined the Our Sunday Visitor family over the years to meet the needs of Catholics in the pew.

Just as Archbishop Noll was always quick to see the potential of new technologies for evangelization, so today his company seeks to use the Internet, radio, CD-ROM, and other communication tools to reach those interested in seeing the world's events through Catholic eyes.

And that small offering envelope company he founded so many years ago? Today, it is the largest Catholic producer of envelopes in the world, helping to teach the principles of Gospel-based stewardship to parishes throughout the country.

One final legacy of Archbishop Noll's passion, energy, and love for the Church is the Our Sunday Visitor Institute. Every year this organization lends financial support to worthy projects, organizations, and conferences that conform in some way to his vision of education, evangelization, and witness. Assistance has been provided throughout the nation and in virtually every diocese.

What Archbishop Noll founded nearly a century ago continues to bear fresh fruit for the sake of the Lord and on behalf of His Church. Following his lead, it remains dedicated to ordinary Catholics who love their Church, love their faith, and strive to live as Jesus commanded them to.

We, the employees of Our Sunday Visitor and the heirs of his mission, are steadfastly committed to Archbishop Noll's original insight: that an educated laity, formed well in the principles of its faith, is not only a lasting bulwark against the temptations of the world but also the most powerful and positive witness to the truths of our Church.

This remains to this day our ministry, the lasting fruit, the continual harvest, sown by this visionary priest, our founder and inspiration: Archbishop John F. Noll.

— GREGORY R. ERLANDSON
PRESIDENT, OUR SUNDAY VISITOR PUBLISHING DIVISION

Preface

John Francis Noll, fifth bishop of Fort Wayne, Indiana, and founder of Our Sunday Visitor, was one of the most influential Catholics of his day. His accomplishments were legion; he made his mark on nearly all of the major Catholic ventures of his time, and many of the institutions and works that he founded or influenced are still thriving today, although he died in 1956. His life spanned one of the most tumultuous periods of American Catholic history, from the era of Pope Pius IX and the First Vatican Council to the threshold of change inspired by Vatican Council II. He lived during a period of unprecedented expansion and immigration in this country, when the American Church was growing exponentially. Catholics in America needed a sense of identity, a sense of self-confidence and pride.

Statue of Archbishop Noll
sculpted by Eugene Kormendi

Noll began to organize and educate an emerging Catholic laity. His was the first Catholic newspaper with national scope, and it signaled the effort to unite American Catholics, bridging the regionalism and ethnic diversity with a corporate identity. A great churchman, Noll was always concerned with the welfare not only of his own diocese, but also of the Church at large. He stands today as the most outstanding Catholic publisher in America.

This book is not a definitive biography. It is not intended as a "brag book" of his accomplishments. Rather, I have tried to paint with words the portrait of the man behind the miter — a man whose works and influence touched millions of American Catholics. He established the ideals for a newspaper and book publishing company with which I have enjoyed working for more than twenty years. It is my hope that the reader of this book will come to better appreciate not only the man who did so much for the Catholics of the United States, but also the humble priest with a strong and simple faith and a generous heart.

— ANN BALL

Introduction

When Americans gather to celebrate national holidays like Thanksgiving and the Fourth of July, we often think about pilgrims landing at Plymouth Rock, English colonists at Jamestown, and the founding fathers gathered in convention in Philadelphia. The early colonists came for many reasons but mostly in search of new lands, prosperity, and religious freedom. The Mayflower Compact in Massachusetts, Roger William's Baptist colony in Providence, Rhode Island, and the Anglicanism of Virginia reflected the impact that Protestant Christianity has made upon the American scene. The results of the "Great Awakenings" helped shape the religious and political character of the nation. The Protestant denominations, which dominated the American landscape, interpreted America's Manifest Destiny to be a result of God's providential plan. America's providential destiny continues to be a powerful force that drives the imagination and affirms the conviction that this is the land of opportunity, freedom, and democracy.

Portrait of Archbishop Noll by Elizabeth Kormendi, hanging at Our Sunday Visitor

From the beginning, American Catholics were considered outsiders in the midst of a predominately Protestant culture. Catholics were suspect because of their perceived loyalty to a foreign power, the Papacy, which had implications not only in religious expression but also in politics. Suspicion of Catholic intentions resulted in periodic displays of anti-Catholicism. Many · questioned whether Catholics could be loyal to the democratic experiment on which the country had been founded. However, Catholics also had arrived seeking religious freedom and the political and economic advantages that the New World offered. They believed that they shared in America's providential destiny. In contrast with their Protestant neighbors, Catholics could boast of their contributions to America's beginnings and growth. They had explored the continent, founded missions, and established settlements. Catholics labored in the task of nation building as farmers, laborers, and soldiers. Therefore, what had once been considered a predominately Protestant nation was soon challenged by the presence of a sizeable Catholic population who began to place their imprint on the landscape of contemporary American life.

John Francis Noll played an instrumental role in the development of American Catholic life and identity. He was born and raised in the heartland of America, a Hoosier from the city of Fort Wayne, of German and Irish heritage. He lived during the first half of the twentieth century, when America was developing its industrial might and flexing its muscle as a world power. This was a time of unprecedented growth and change for the nation and the Church. He witnessed the impact of the world at war, the Depression, and the advent of the atomic age. As immigrants poured into the country by the tens of thousands, many were Catholics who came from Ireland, Germany, Italy, Eastern Europe, and Mexico. Their cultural diversity presented a unique challenge in the Church's effort to educate and assimilate them into American Catholic life.

As a Catholic priest, and later as Bishop of Fort Wayne, John Noll was the editor of the national Catholic weekly, *Our Sunday*

Visitor. He believed that the Catholic Church must claim its providential role in the shaping of America. Through his paper and his numerous books and pamphlets, he spoke to a nation of Catholics to educate them in their faith and promote the spirit of Catholic Action. He organized his readers — "the Friends of Our Sunday Visitor," as he called them — to be the catalyst for the work of the Church. He shared with them the belief that by being good Catholics, they were also being good, loyal Americans. For a largely immigrant population, this became an important part of their assimilation into American life. As an accomplished apologist, Noll also presented the teachings of the Catholic faith to Protestants and demonstrated to them that Catholicism was not incompatible with American ideals.

John Noll was a missionary at heart, whose influence extended through the printed word and his work as a bishop in the Catholic hierarchy. Through his leadership and strength of character, he aspired to educate against religious bigotry, racism, and prejudice. He fought anti-Catholicism in all its forms. He promoted the values of a nation based on the principle of "One Nation Under God." In a time of mounting secularism and materialism, he encouraged the principles of marriage and family life and urged that education and politics be rooted in religious truths. He supported the rights of labor and capital and the care of immigrants. He raised awareness against the enemies of society by working for public decency in movies and magazines and showed a deep concern for America's youth. He strongly opposed the spread of atheistic Communism and totalitarian governments that used war and social unrest to threaten the progress of Church and society.

This is the story of a man who committed his life to the Christian principles that made him a faithful Catholic and a loyal American. He was industrious and dedicated to the American spirit of tolerance and civility. Like many of his contemporary bishops, who were builders with "brick and mortar," Archbishop Noll also used his numerous skills to organize and advance the apostolate of the laity to be a catalyst for the good of the Church and society. As the "Harmonizer," a title associated with his paper, he promoted an America rooted in the firm conviction "In God We Trust." As an American and Catholic, then, John Francis Noll was right on the money.

— FR. LEON HUTTON

CHAPTER ONE

———◄○►———

THAT'S A LIE!

That, sir, is a bare-faced lie!"

Shaking with anger, his face flushed as red as the hair on his head, a sturdy young priest jumped to his feet and challenged a man at the front of the room. It was 1901, and Fr. John Noll, in the company of a few other priests, was attending an anti-Catholic talk at Island Park in Rome City, Indiana, given by a certain Rev. F.F. De Long.

Talks of this sort, directed against Catholics, were popular at the time. Based on intolerance and black, unreasoning hatred, the talks purported to "expose" the immorality and false religion of the Catholic Church. For the audience, primarily simply badly informed country people, the lectures provided something to do to alleviate the boredom of a Friday night in a small country town with little means of entertainment. But unfortunately, sometimes the alleged "outrages of the Papists" caused audiences to become so inflamed that they went out and rioted. For the organizers of these sessions, however, there was a substantial financial reward from entry fees and collections; largely unchallenged in their assertions, they didn't

Young Fr. Noll

care much about the consequences of what they said or how they said it.

That was all about to change.

"Mr. DeLong," Noll continued, "you have just said that gross immorality is the general rule in our convents, and you allege that these things don't leak out because we priests are the only ones permitted inside a convent. That's a lie, Mr. DeLong!"

"I can substantiate that assertion," DeLong retorted. "I'll give you fifty dollars if you'll get me inside a certain convent I shall name in Fort Wayne."

At that, Fr. Quinlan, pastor of the cathedral parish in Fort Wayne, stood up beside Noll.

"I'm a pastor in Fort Wayne," he said. "We'll take you up on your offer. Hand your wager to one of the committee members up there on the podium with you, and I'll even pay your way. We'll go to Fort Wayne, and I'll make certain you are allowed to inspect any convent you wish!"

Seeing that his bluff had been called, DeLong immediately began to backpedal, stating that he couldn't break God's commandment against gambling. But, having regained the floor, he quickly concluded the evening with an invitation to his next talk, two days later. At that time, he said, he would prove his allegations by appearing with an ex-priest ready to detail the horrors of the "Church of Rome."

Fr. Noll, of course, was one of the first to arrive at the next lecture. With disgust, he heard more of the same misrepresentation, with the "ex-priest Delaney" painting a lurid picture of the wickedness of his fellow priests which resulted in his leaving the priesthood. He spoke at length of a priest named Chiniquy and his supposed depredations. These bigoted, hateful, and untrue remarks whipped the audience into a frenzy to the point that young John Noll was afraid some would grab up baseball bats or other weapons and go to seek out the closest "nest of Romans," as some people called Catholics.

But Fr. Noll had done his homework. He had with him notes on DeLong's unsavory reputation, including a letter from the preacher's wife saying that DeLong had attempted to kill her by forcing her to drink carbolic acid. From comments the man made during his speech, Fr. Noll also knew that Delaney had never been a priest. But he had no intention of attempting to inform the henchmen of their errors; it was the audience that needed to be convinced. Delaney had to be discredited. So, politely, Fr. Noll waited until the end of the lecture and then arose to take the floor.

"What diocese are you from, sir?" he called out to the self-styled former priest.

The man responded, "Chicago."

Nodding, Fr. Noll turned and addressed the audience directly. "My dear people, I am a priest myself, the pastor at Kendallville, and I happen to know that your speaker has never been a priest. It is true that the Fr. Chiniquy[1] was a priest, but he was booted out of the ministry for misconduct. But Mr. Delaney has never been a priest. Let me ask him a single question, and you can judge for yourself. Mr. Delaney, what is an Ordo?"

There was a dead silence in the auditorium as all eyes turned to hear Delaney's answer. After thirty long seconds, Noll repeated his question, "What is an Ordo?" Still, the supposed former priest did not answer, so Mr. DeLong leapt into the fray.

"That's not fair," he cried. "Mr. Delaney has been out of the Catholic ministry for many years. You can't expect him to remember these technical terms when he never uses them!"

"Very well. Let me remind you what an Ordo is," boomed out the young priest. "It's the annotated calendar found on the desk of every priest. A priest consults it every day. Remember?"

Again turning to the audience, Fr. Noll continued, "Now, tomorrow night, it's my turn to talk. You have spent the entire night hearing a liar, pretending to be a priest, telling you a lot of nonsense about the Catholic Church. I'm giving you a chance to hear a real priest tell you the truth. I'll be on that very stage tomorrow night. If you are fair-minded, you'll come. *No admission charge or collection will be needed.* That's for men like DeLong and Delaney. And you will all be free to ask as many questions as you like."

True to his word, the following night Fr. Noll spoke and answered questions to a full house. Unknowingly, the priest was embarking on a lifetime mission of education, one in which he would defend his faith in the face of the anti-Catholic bigotry and slander of his day and use the power of his pen to educate his own people who were often equally ill informed about the tenets of their own religion.

CHAPTER TWO

---◄◊►---

EARLY DAYS

John Noll had his roots firmly planted deep in the rich Indiana soil. The Noll family had settled in the then sleepy little farming community of Fort Wayne in 1834, when his grandfather, George Johannes Noll, a tailor, emigrated from Germany. The family rode in a wagon from Detroit, Michigan, over an almost impassible road, as there was no railroad or waterway to get to Fort Wayne.

His father, John George Noll, one of three brothers, was born in Fort Wayne in 1841. John's mother, Anna Ford, was born in 1843 in London, England, of Irish parents. She came to America as a young girl and married John George about 1864. The young couple immediately began to raise a family. John George held a number of occupations: he ran a haberdashery, worked as a grocer, and at one time was a bookkeeper on the staff of the comptroller for the city of Fort Wayne. He also served as a city councilman. Anna had her hands full with the care of the babies who arrived almost annually: Mary Elizabeth, Catherine, George, William, little Eugene (who died as a baby), John, and Loretto.

John was born January 25, 1875, in a house on East Lewis Street, next to the house where his father had been born. A week later, baby John, the sixth child of the lively Noll brood, was baptized at the Cathedral church in Fort Wayne, where his own father had been baptized thirty-four years previously.

When little Johnny was a baby, the Noll clan dominated East Lewis Street. Since his grandfather arrived two decades before, the family had grown to the point that, by the 1860s, the Noll

name took up nearly half a page of the city directory. John's grandfather lived in the corner house; and on the other side his two uncles, Martin and Frank, lived with their families. A solidly Catholic family, John's first cousin Raymond (Frank's son) also entered the priesthood and became the Vicar General of the Archdiocese of Indianapolis. John's stepsister Evelyn became a Sister of Providence.

When Johnny was only three and a half years old, his mother died of consumption (tuberculosis) at the early age

Baby John, 1875

of 32. The youngest of the six surviving Noll children, Loretto, was only five months old at the time. John George knew that his children needed a mother's care and married his housekeeper within a year, in 1880. His second wife was young Mary Josephine McCleary of Bluffton. Seventeen years younger than her husband, and only seven years older than her oldest stepchild, she was to have a large influence on little Johnny.

Mary had been educated by the Sisters of the Holy Cross at Sacred Heart Academy near Fort Wayne. Earlier a Protestant, she converted to the Catholic Church and became known for her mature faith. It is probable that her Protestant background influenced young John's later lively interest in explaining the faith to non-Catholics. He had a lifelong interest in conversions and was always happy to bring a new soul into the Church. Mary and John George had eleven other children: Joseph, Effie, Walter, Thomas, Melissa, Gertrude, Muriel, Georgia, Marcelline, Evelyn, and Velma.

Johnny started school at age five, at the Cathedral Elementary School taught by the Brothers of the Holy Cross. At the end of his eighth grade year, when he was thirteen years old, he made his First Communion and was confirmed, May 20, 1888. (First Communions were celebrated later in that era.)

That June, he took a job at the M. Frank Dry Goods store, working from 6 A.M. to 6 P.M., Monday through Saturday, for a salary of two dollars per week.

For some time, young John had been thinking of a vocation to the priesthood. Although several of the others boys in his class had talked abut this lofty ideal, it was an intensely personal subject to John, who kept his thoughts to himself, thinking it was possibly only a youthful dream. For several years he had been a faithful altar server, and as he joined in the center of the Catholic liturgy, he thought more and more about his own vocation. Although he didn't speak of becoming a priest, others noticed his attitude.

During the summer after his graduation, John often served Mass for Fr. Thomas O'Leary, the assistant at the Cathedral who had prepared him for First Holy Communion. One day the priest asked him if he had ever thought of studying for the priesthood. Thoughtfully, John replied, "Yes, I have thought about it often this past year. Honestly, I have just been waiting for someone to tell me how to arrange it and where to go."

Immediately, the priest set about making arrangements to get John ready to leave the first week in September for St. Lawrence of Brundisium Minor Seminary in Mt. Calvary, Wisconsin, conducted by the Capuchin Fathers. Although John had never seen a Capuchin, he had heard of the austerity of their life and the rigorous program at the seminary. He was willing, however, to face any hardship to reach his goal of the priesthood.

Archbishop Noll's coat of arms, featuring his motto *Mentes Tuorum Visita*.
Taken from the hymn *Veni Creator Spiritus*, the words literally translate
as an invitation to the Holy Spirit to "visit [or *appear to*]
the minds of your people."

CHAPTER THREE

Minor Seminary — a Rugged Trial

When young John Noll entered the seminary in Mount Calvary, Wisconsin, he entered a whole new world. With so many
younger brothers and sisters at home, John had never been
spoiled. He was a hard worker and used to taking care of himself.
Still, nothing had prepared him for the rigors of life at St.
Lawrence Minor Seminary. In spite of the austerity, though, this
was a place where boys developed lifelong friendships; the difficulties bonded them together and formed a new set of "brothers."

A strict schedule, based on that of many religious orders, was
followed. Each morning the students awoke at 5:30 A.M., washed
and dressed in silence and filed out for the short walk to the local
church. Here, they had a period of Morning Prayer and medita-
tion before daily Mass. During the winter, that meant kneeling for
an hour in a very cold church, shivering in spite of their heavy
clothing, as the church was only heated on the weekends.

After Mass, the boys returned to their upstairs dormitory to
make their beds and prepare for the day. There were no modern
conveniences at the seminary, not even running water, so the boys
took turns bringing water in buckets from an outside well to their
third floor dormitory to fill the wash basins on the stand by each
bed. Also in turns, they took large baskets of dirty clothes each

week to the sisters' convent three blocks away. At the end of the week, they returned to the convent for the clean laundry.

During their morning work, the boys maintained complete silence lasting through their meager breakfast — a thick slice of bread and coffee made from roasted barley. Afterward, the boys could relax for half an hour while getting ready for morning classes.

For ten minutes before noon, the boys gathered in the chapel for a daily examination of conscience, kneeling in earnest soul searching. During lunch, one of the students read selections from a pious book in the refectory; no one was allowed to talk or visit over their plain, but healthful, food. Afternoon classes were followed by an hour of recreation. The boys gathered again in chapel to recite the Rosary and for spiritual reading before supper. Just as at lunch, supper was eaten to the accompaniment of more pious reading. After a final hour of recreation, the boys studied until night prayer and lights out at nine.

There was no daily contact with life outside the seminary. These young teenagers aspiring to the priesthood led a life of study and contemplation. No newspapers or magazines were allowed, no one left the grounds without permission, and the sports were intramural. It was a hard life and must have been difficult for the boys who came from large and loving families. Undoubtedly, many tears of homesickness were shed in the dark of the silent dormitory at night. School lasted from September to the end of June. For the five years that John studied at St. Lawrence, he only returned home during the school year once. During Christmas of his first year, his six-year-old sister Effie died, so John was allowed to visit with his family during this time, and to attend her funeral.

For John, far more daunting than the rigorous schedule at St. Lawrence was the fact that most of the instruction, and almost all of the textbooks, were in German. His grandfather spoke German, but John had never studied the language. Although the task seems almost impossible to modern students, John not only learned German, but also Latin, French, and Greek at the same time. At times, the hours he spent preparing for class seemed hopelessly inadequate. John would wake in the darkness and, stumbling to the washbasin, splash his face with the frigid water, hoping to clear the mists from his brain. At night, he threw himself on his bed, exhausted.

The young seminarian

Daily he struggled through his course in Classics. He read and studied the works of Nepos, Caesar, Livy, Cicero, and Horace, in Latin, and Xenephon and Homer in Greek. He also studied Ovid and Virgil and the great philosophers like Augustine, Aquinas, Abelard, Peter Lombard, and others, and the Christian spiritual classics.

Proof that his efforts paid off is the fact that he finished his five years of preparatory seminary as an honor student with near perfect marks in all subjects. In his final year there, 1892-93, John took courses in Christian Doctrine, Latin, Greek, English, Rhetoric, Geometry, Physics, History, and French. He received all I's (very good), and graduated third in his class.

Like most of the boys at St. Lawrence, John became a member of the Third Order of St. Francis. With them, he regularly recited the Little Office of the Blessed Virgin during the day. Because of this, he learned many of the breviary prayers by memory. Following the Mass with the Latin missal, he also was familiar with the entire Latin text of the Ordinary of the Mass before he entered major seminary at the age of nineteen.

The hardships of minor seminary served as a test for the students' vocation, and John Noll passed with flying colors. Later, he treasured the fact that he had been forced to learn German and French, as both languages helped him in his work as a parish priest. The Indiana immigrants from these countries were much more comfortable making their confession in their native language, and young Fr. Noll often said a few words at Mass in these languages.

CHAPTER FOUR

MAJOR SEMINARY — CLOSER TO THE GOAL

At last, it was time to go to Mt. St. Mary's Seminary in Cincinnati, Ohio, to complete his studies for the priesthood. With happy anticipation, John and his family began preparing the things he would need to take with him. He was fitted for a tailored cassock, made of heavy serge, with deep cuffs and pockets in all sorts of mysterious places. He also ordered a clerical vest, biretta, and a dozen Roman collars. His second mother, Mary, sewed his surplices by hand. His family delighted in seeing young Johnny, dressed in the clerical garb he would wear as a major seminarian, on his way to the priesthood.

John entered the seminary on September 14, 1893. After the hard years at St. Lawrence, the atmosphere of the seminary seemed much more relaxed. Although the discipline was strict, each seminarian had a private room, and on free days students were allowed to go sightseeing in the city with fellow students.

All of the theology lectures were given in Latin, and the students were

The "first five," John's oldest siblings

required to answer their questions in that language. Here John's thinking, speaking, and writing became concise and powerful, and he developed a clear and logical way of thinking. At the end of his second year of philosophy, John won the class competition and received as a prize a six-volume set of St. Thomas' *Summa Philosophica.*

During his study of theology, John became devoted to apologetics — proving the logical position of the Catholic Church. His studies were intense, but interesting, and the weeks seemed to fly past as the young seminarian matured from boyhood to manhood.

Out on the Farm

During the summers, John often spent his vacation time at the Herman Schnelker farm near New Haven, or visiting at the Besancon rectory with his friend Fr. Francis LaBonte. (It was common for seminarians to find hospitality in a parish or private home for the summer.)

By the second summer break, John was exhausted from his strenuous studies and physically spent. He wrote his friend Ed Schnelker and begged him to ask his parents if he could visit for a couple of weeks to drink a lot of fresh milk and build himself

John and friends

back up. The answer, of course, was "yes." But, unfortunately, the Schnelkers didn't realize how run-down the young man was. Since John had been there before and would remember his way to the farm, the boys didn't bother hitching their horse, "Old Tom," to the buggy to go and meet him at the Wabash station.

The entire family was shocked when John finally knocked at the door. After the long walk from the station, he was so exhausted that he couldn't speak over a whisper and immediately asked if he could lie down for a short rest. Scolding her sons for not meeting John, Mrs. Schnelker immediately began to bustle about to find ways to help build the young man's strength back up.

The Schnelkers had a windmill and pump for the well in back of their house to draw up fresh, cool water. At first, while the Schnelker boys greedily drank several cups of the refreshing water from the old tin cup by the well, John could only slurp a table-spoon or two. And when he tried to help the boys with their harvest chores, he was still too weak to do much. As Mr. Schnelker operated the self-binder on the hay, the boys would gather up the golden sheaves of grain, stacking them into shocks. The Schnelker boys cheerfully hoisted two or three sheaves at a time, while poor John was barely able to lift a single one.

But soon, the loving care of his friends began to show, and he regained strength rapidly. By the end of the summer, his health had returned, and he was able to help saw down an old pine tree in the front yard. Then, with saw and ax, the boys chopped the tree into kitchen-stove-length pieces and kindling, and hauled it to the wood shed in a wheelbarrow.

As John's strength returned, so did his voice, and he began to practice his preaching to the trees in the orchard. John talked so loud the Schnelker brothers worried that someone might notice him and think he had gone daft, so they suggested it might be better to practice in the barn, preaching to the walls instead of the trees. John readily complied, and the brothers sneaked around and often peeked through the cracks of the barn to hear him declaiming. They enjoyed watching him practice dramatic gestures — and more than one of his practice sermons hit home with them.

The brothers mentioned John's speeches to some friends and the word spread through the small town that the Schnelkers had a good speaker visiting at their home. A Protestant man named Effie got a gang of fellows together and came up to the farm and asked the Schnelker boys if they would ask their guest to give them a talk. John readily agreed and, using stack of hay between the barns as a pulpit, he gave a lively speech. Years later, Effie remembered that as the best sermon he ever heard.

Fr. Bernard Wiedau, a very pious man, was then the pastor of St. John's Church at New Haven. On Sundays, the youth sat at the front of the church on straight benches with no backrest. Fr. Wiedau would read the epistle, the gospel, and then preach the sermon, first in German, then in French, and finally in English, in his concern for his multi-ethnic parish. In spite of his watchful eye, occasionally one of the youth would fall asleep during the long, extended sermon, and topple backwards off the bench. The Mass, which began at 10 A.M., was rarely finished before noon.

The first time John went to confession to the pious old priest, by the time he left the confessional, his face was redder than his hair — he was so embarrassed that others in line would think he was a truly great sinner. As he knelt to say his penance, however, he noticed that the others stayed equally as long, so his mind eased a bit on that score. By the time he returned to the farm afterward, he could joke about it with the boys.

Young Fr. LaBonte, stationed at nearby Besancon, was the proud possessor of a two-wheeled sulky. By the simple expedient of putting a board across the single seat, two could ride in place of one. John and the Schnelker brothers were often treated to a ride in this way.

CHAPTER FIVE

THOU ART A PRIEST FOREVER

During Passion Week of 1898, the same year that Teddy Roosevelt and Admiral Dewey were fighting the Spanish-American War, young John Noll received the Subdiaconate with the traditional pledge of celibacy. He made his vow before Archbishop William Henry Elder of Cincinnati and received the Diaconate the following day. Immediately, preparations for his ordination were made.

On June 4, 1898, at the early age of 23, John Noll was ordained at the Cathedral of Fort Wayne by Bishop Joseph Rademacher. Originally, a later date had been set, but two compelling reasons caused the date to be changed. First, the gravely ill rector of the Cathedral, Fr. Joseph Brammer, greatly desired to see the ordination of this first seminarian from his parish to be ordained. He feared he would not live until the end of the month, so the Bishop honored his final wish. The second reason was a request by Fr. Henry Boecklemann, who had known John

Ordination day

when he was an elementary school student. A diabetic, Fr. Boecklemann planned to take a vacation to rest and wanted John to take his place.

Fr. Brammer himself made the preparations for the First

A priest at last, 1898

Mass, to be celebrated on June 5, the feast of the Holy Trinity. He carefully selected a speaker, Msgr. Joseph Kroll, a respected preacher, and two young girls dressed in white to lead the procession to the altar. He also arranged for a large parish reception following the Mass. Afterward, the tired but happy priest went to his bed, never to leave it again. His premonition was correct — he died on June 20.

At the banquet following the reception, John noticed his friends the Schnelkers seated at the end of the table. The young priest got up and went to bring them to sit next to him at the head of the table. His parents were on one side; these close friends on the other. As a gift, they presented John with a nice watch, which — many years later — he returned as a gift to one of their sons.

CHAPTER SIX

A MISSION BEGINS

Less than a week after ordination, the young priest found himself on the train to the far northern part of the state, to the city of Elkhart, to serve as a temporary replacement for the ailing Fr. Boecklemann. Here he was to have full charge of the parish of 150 families while the pastor was gone, a daunting assignment for young Fr. Noll.

Eagerly he walked to the church on Main Street. He smiled as he saw the handsome house next door, which he assumed must be the rectory. When he rang the bell and announced to the friendly sister who answered that he had come to take Fr. Boecklemann's place while he was gone, he received the first of many shocks he would experience in Elkhart. Instead of welcoming him

The young priest at home

inside, the sister led him to a series of ramshackle wooden buildings, each hardly larger than a shed, behind the church near the railroad tracks. Fr. Boecklemann had turned his rectory over to the sisters of the Holy Cross for a convent, and he and his mother had moved into the poor quarters behind the church.

As he ruefully surveyed the unpainted shack with holes in the wall, wondering if it leaked when it rained, the sister smilingly informed him that the hoboes wouldn't bother him.

"H-Hoboes?" he stammered. Seeing the look of surprise on his face, she hastened to explain that often when the trains passed by, these wanderers jumped off and headed for what were apparently deserted shacks to sleep a while. Telling the young priest that if he gave them a little food then *he* wouldn't bother *them*, she left him to get washed up before exploring the rest of his new domain.

On Saturday, Fr. Noll entered the little church apprehensively to hear his first confessions. Fortunately, there were only a few in line, and all went well. The seminary professors had prepared him well for all contingencies and, by the end of the day, the eager young priest found himself wishing for more penitents as an outlet for his zeal. The following day, his first sermons also went smoothly. Two Masses were needed to accommodate all the worshippers, and the rules allowed for the priest to say both in such a case. However, since he could not break his fast from the previous midnight until both were said, Fr. Noll found himself very hungry by the end of the second Mass. After lunch he counted the meager collection. It was just short of six dollars, most of it in pennies.

Then Fr. Noll prepared for the baptism that was set for two in the afternoon. The ceremony flowed along until he came to the imposition of salt. At the taste, the infant began squalling in its godmother's arms until it worked itself into a full-fledged tantrum. The rest of the service the baby screamed so loudly that it rattled the young priest badly, and when he finished, the christening party was nearly out of the church before he remembered to call them back to get the information needed for the baptismal registry.

In the seven months Fr. Noll served at Elkhart, time passed quickly for the young priest. In addition to his priestly duties, during the weekdays he walked throughout the parish — which covered the entire city — visiting the families and getting to know his people. By nightfall he was exhausted, happy to get to bed early because his days began early. Although he was often called out on sick calls at night, there was not a single death of any of his parishioners during his time there. He did, however, attend the deathbed to give last rites to one of the tramps at the County Poor House between Elkhart and Goshen.

One night, Fr. Noll was roused from sleep by the screams of Fr. Boecklemann's elderly mother, who still lived at the rectory with him. A tramp had broken in and, finding the 86-year-old woman awake, grabbed her by the neck and threatened to choke her if she made any noise. She screamed anyway, frightening off the intruder before the sleepy priest could give chase and catch him.

The first week of September, the diocesan clergy went on an eight-day retreat. Fr. Noll had just made a retreat before his ordination, so he was called by the Bishop to help a religious order priest take care of the Cathedral parish for those eight days. It was a hectic week. He answered sick calls in seven surrounding towns, traveling by train or horse and buggy. On the evening before First Friday, he and the other priest heard confessions from two in the afternoon until midnight. Just as the weary priest was headed for bed, he was called to attend a dying woman in Wabash, forty-five miles away. He took the next train and, when he arrived, was met by the lady's son at the station.

But when he came to the dying woman's home, Fr. Noll learned that the priest had already anointed her before he left for the retreat. "I just thought there might be some rite of the Church I hadn't received yet," she said innocently.

Feeling he should at least give her Communion, he walked the mile to the local church — only to find that the priest had consumed all the consecrated hosts before he'd left. By this time, it was three in the morning, and the next train for Fort Wayne left at five. He arrived back just in time for the eight o'clock Mass at the cathedral for the hundreds who wanted to receive Holy Communion on First Friday. He finished in a state of near collapse, since he hadn't eaten since early the evening before.

That Christmas, the first in his ministry, Fr. Noll found vastly different from any he had ever spent. On Christmas Eve, he kept busy decorating the church. Large spruce trees were set in place over a beautiful crib scene placed on cotton to represent snow. The altars and windows were festooned with evergreens. All afternoon and evening was spent in "the box," hearing the confessions of the scores of people who wanted to attend Christmas Mass. Not only the devout, but also those who only attended church on the major feasts, shuffled their feet in the long line before the confessionals.

Christmas Day, Fr. Noll offered the first of three Masses at five in the morning. After the third Mass, he returned to the rectory and took up his breviary to pray. Suddenly, something seemed wrong. The house was too quiet. With shock, he realized he missed the happy laughter and excitement of children on this, a day devoted to children. The twenty-four-year-old had finally stopped and paused in his busy schedule long enough to realize he was lonely. He missed the loving warmth of his large family. He gazed at the crucifix hanging over his bed, taking consolation from One whose sacrifice was greater than his own, and silently and somberly returned to his prayers.

In Elkhart, there were only a few Catholics compared to the number of Protestants, so there were many mixed marriages. There could be only two results of such a marriage: either the

Church lost a member, or it gained the children and, sometimes, the non-Catholic spouse. Hoping for the latter result, Fr. Noll tried to explain more about the Church to those coming for marriage instruction. Almost immediately, he began to encounter a great deal of blind prejudice against the Church; not only the Protestants were ignorant, but many Catholics themselves did not understand their own Church.

Here, in this little woebegone rectory in a Protestant area of northern Indiana, Fr. John Noll began to realize what would be the greatest part of his life's work — the explanation of the beautiful truths of the Catholic faith to Catholics and Protestants alike, clearly and *in words they all could understand.*

Most Protestants knew little about the Catholic Church. Simply average people, most of those who criticized the Church did not act from malice — they only suffered from a lack of real knowledge. Few of them had failed to hear the whispered calumny of the weird happenings in the priesthood, the Latin "hocus pocus"[2] of the Mass, and the strange and perverted sexual peccadilloes of the priests, who kept nuns prisoner in convents for their own pleasure... and more.

Frauds and liars posing as ex-priests and ex-nuns, like the infamous Maria Monk, traveled the countryside making a good living from giving lectures and regaling their audiences with stories of violence and lust.

There weren't enough priests to challenge them on their own grounds. And, Fr. Noll realized sadly, his own people didn't — couldn't — help. They, too, were ignorant of much of the history and tradition of their own Catholic Church. In this frontier area, few had received any education above the elementary grades. Nothing was written in

Actual photo of the fake nun "Maria Monk" and one of her illegitimate children the ordinary language of the people to explain the truth and beauty of the Catholic faith.

Clearly, something had to be done. But what could he — one man — do?

Fr. Noll could not tell enough in his weekly sermon to help. He picked up a pen and began to scribble a few words . . . "A message from your pastor." Looking at what he had written, he began to laugh at himself. What a foolish idea. He couldn't very well write a letter to each of his parishioners, or to each of the Protestants in the town, much less in the country. So he continued to pray, and to think.

He prayed his rosary as he tramped up and down the aisles of the church, always thinking. He must find a way to break down this wall that kept so many souls from God. The wall of ignorance haunted him and he began to attack it the best way he knew how — with prayer and logical thought.

God's Nomad

In January, the Bishop told Fr. Noll to go to Logansport to fill in for the pastor there, who was recovering from typhoid fever. The young priest began to realize that, in many ways, his life would mimic that of the hoboes back in Elkhart. He might have to move at any time and would have to travel light. This, too, was part of the sacrifice he was willingly making for love of his God.

The weather in Logansport was miserable; for more than a month the temperature hovered below zero. St. Brigid's was heated with natural gas but, because of the heavy demand for fuel, few places were really warm, including the rectory. There was no heat at all in Fr. Noll's bedroom. Nightly, the housekeeper filled a pitcher with water so the young priest could wash up in the morning. The first morning of the cold spell, however, he awoke to a pitcher of ice. The cold snap was so severe that Fr. Noll was kept busy with sick calls to parishioners suffering from pneumonia.

One freezing day, Fr. Noll was called to bring the last rites to a patient at the Long Cliff Institution for the Insane. Fearing she was near death, her relatives had asked for the priest. The woman had been a patient for 23 years, and the nurse informed him that in all her own years at the asylum, the lady had never had a lucid moment. She assured the young priest that the woman wouldn't even know why he was there.

As they stood by the bed, Fr. Noll's heart leapt at a surprise display of divine grace. Slowly, the woman folded her hands, and her lips began to move in

The young pastor in 1908

prayer. Quickly, Fr. Noll shooed the nurse from the room and asked the patient if she would like to confess. She responded well, and he was able to finish the rite just as he would have with any normal person. The nurse returned when it was time to give Viaticum and the anointing.

As Fr. Noll approached with the Eucharist, the woman seemed particularly reverent and extended her tongue to receive. The astonished nurse told Fr. Noll that the woman had refused to taste any food for the previous few days. He left with a happy heart, full of the wonder of a God who restored His child to perfect consciousness and allowed her to die in His loving embrace.

A Young Pastor

Within less than a year of his ordination, and at only 24 years of age, Fr. Noll was named pastor of St. Patrick's at Ligonier. The sprawling parish covered thirty square miles and included two missions, Kendallville and Millersburg. This was Protestant country, where the Catholics were a small minority. Ligonier was primarily a Jewish settlement. Fr. Noll actually arrived on the train with the local rabbi. Ironically, the rabbi was also a redhead, who kindly showed him to the home of one of the four Catholic families who lived in the city.

Conditions in Ligonier were primitive. The rectory was heated by a small soft coal stove. The temperature was twenty below zero on the day he arrived and, going to the basement for some coal, he discovered that all the coal was encased in a block of solid ice. He had to laugh at the fact that his first job was as a coal miner, using the tools he found in the basement to chip out enough coal for a fire.

Once a fire was started, Fr. Noll discovered the stove had a defective grate so he had to become a mechanic to fix a way to prop it so that all the coals wouldn't wind up in the ash pan. The church, too, was in bad repair, with the wallpaper dangling from the walls and ceiling in places. The archaic stoves in the church gave off more smoke than heat, and at Mass he could barely see the parishioners for the haze. He knew they were there, though, because of the constant choking coughs during the liturgy.

The church was heated only on Sunday, so for weekly Mass he staved off frostbite by the simple expedient of wrapping two heated bricks and placing them at either side of the corporal where he could occasionally place his hands to warm them.

The people were generous and gave what they could, but because it was an economically depressed area, and because there were so few Catholics, there was never an abundance of money to cover the needed costs, much less such luxuries as a housekeeper. So, during his tenure at this parish, Fr. Noll made many needed repairs, had the interior of the church nicely redecorated, and put in a different heating system.

In addition to all the work of the parish and its two missions, Fr. Noll became his own housekeeper, janitor, and — worst of all — cook. Coming from a large family, he was self-reliant in most areas; however, like many another single man before him, he had no training in the culinary arts.

Fr. Noll soon developed his own unique recipe for a boiled dinner that saved time and used only a single pan. He would throw a few ears of corn into the pan, add a can of pork and beans, and finish by stirring in a couple of eggs. There is no record that anyone who ever joined him for lunch ever asked for the recipe.

Because of the preponderance of Protestants, many of his new neighbors were greatly misinformed about the Catholic Church. Fr. Noll loved to talk religion and patiently explained the tenets of his faith to anyone willing to listen. However, there were times when he and his listener would politely agree to disagree. That was the case when a devout Adventist neighbor paid him a welcoming call in his early days at Ligonier. A few days later, Noll paid a return call and discovered he had arrived just at the beginning of a meeting of Adventists, who regularly held their services in the man's home.

The man was surprised, but then politely welcomed Fr. Noll, introduced him to the gathering, and invited him to lead the group in prayer. Totally unprepared, Noll began to recite a popular prayer to the Holy Family as if he were making it up himself. At the end of the first part, which invokes Christ's blessings, a number of the Adventists piped up with "Amen!" or "Amen, brother!" But then, as he continued, invoking the Virgin Mary and St. Joseph, there was an immediate hush followed by a few grumbles. Blushing with embarrassment, Fr. Noll tactfully apologized for disturbing their meeting, praised their earnestness and zeal, and withdrew quickly.

A retired Methodist minister supplemented his pension by selling "edifying" books and approached Fr. Noll to purchase a pricey set of history books. According to the prospectus, one of the volumes dealt with the Reformation. Fr. Noll asked the man to be allowed to look at one of the books before purchasing them. When the minister arrived back with the sample volume, he assured Fr. Noll that the books were very fair to Catholics.

Opening the book, Fr. Noll immediately encountered the sentence, "An indulgence is a license to sin for a remuneration." When he read the sentence aloud, the minister replied that he didn't know what the young priest personally taught, but that that was the universally accepted definition of an indulgence.

Laughing, Fr. Noll replied, "I teach what the Church teaches. And if the Catholic Church taught any such rot, Luther and his followers would have been joined in their revolt by Catholics everywhere." Nonetheless, he purchased the books. With his interest in apologetics, he wanted to see what the opposition was printing in order to be able to more effectively combat the untruths.

One of Fr. Noll's first tasks at Ligonier was to take a census of the Catholics in his parish. He began to visit each family, walking or riding horseback. He soon came to the conclusion that it would be more practical for him to live in Kendallville, where the majority of the Catholic families were located in the city, rather than Ligonier, where they were spread out around the surrounding countryside. His schedule of Masses in the parish and its two missions was dictated by the train schedule; when he was late at Kendallville, he slept in the sacristy, since there was no rectory there.

Fr. Noll knew, however, that he couldn't just suggest a move to Kendallville to the Ligonier parishioners. The previous pastor had alienated the people of Ligonier by moving to Kendallville without their advice or support, and Fr. Noll himself had been brought in to appease the people and restore confidence in their pastor. After a year, he hit on a clever plan. He wrote a letter to the administrator of the diocese, outlining the logical reasons for such a switch.

The Vicar General saw the good sense in the arguments and simply copied them onto his official stationery, along with the order of the transfer of the priest "for the good of souls." Fr. Noll read this letter from the pulpit and, although there was some audible grumbling from the congregation, the supreme authority of the Diocese had spoken, and no one pursued the matter.

Fr. Noll regularly celebrated a Saturday Mass at Millersburg. Sunday Masses were celebrated at Ligonier and Kendallville. There was only one train to the mission at Millersburg, 28 miles away, which left at five in the morning. It arrived at six, leaving him with time on his hands before the service. To fill the time, he walked to a home about a mile from the station where an aged couple lived with two young great-grandchildren. Fr. Noll gave religious instruction to the children, leaving in time to walk back into town for the nine o'clock Mass.

Once, Fr. Noll decided to go to Millersburg the night before his Saturday morning Mass and give the people in town a chance to learn some of the Catholic beliefs. He put a notice of the lecture, set for 7:30 Friday evening, in the weekly paper circulated in the area. When he arrived, there were only a few Catholics in the church. Within a few minutes, however, it seemed as if the entire town arrived in parade. They came in groups, all apparently afraid to come alone. They filled the body of the church and the sanctuary, and since it was a pleasant evening, the rest listened from the lawn outside the open windows.

Fr. Noll spoke for 45 minutes, which he thought adequate. However, seeing that the audience was so attentive and seemed to want to hear more, he continued for another 45 minutes. Later reports from his parishioners said the town's reaction was favorable and that he'd proven quite helpful in explaining some of the beliefs of their Faith to the Protestants. Soon, two non-Catholic women who had married Catholic men came to him and

An early note to a convert

requested instructions. They and their seven children were all baptized at once, which filled the heart of the young priest with joy.

Because of the anti-Catholic climate of the times, and the
gross misrepresentations of the Church by speakers pretending
to be former priests, Fr. Noll decided to give a series of talks on
the Faith at his church on Sunday nights. He invited all the
Protestants of the area, and they responded well. Pastor Rose and
some of the trustees of the local Church of Christ attended one
of the talks. On their way home, one of the trustees suggested
that the pastor respond to Fr. Noll. Pastor Rose did preach a single sermon in rejoinder, but, seeing that Fr. Noll's lectures were
being given to a full house each week, he challenged Father to a
public debate. He issued his initial challenge both by special mes-
senger to the priest and in the newspaper.

A lively correspondence between the two ensued, which
ended abruptly when Pastor Rose suggested they charge an
admission fee to cover the cost of having a stenographer record
the debate. Fr. Noll objected, saying that people might think they
were only trying to raise money. At that, instead of answering
personally, the pastor put his reply in the newspaper: "Let me tell
Fr. Noll that the Roman Catholic Church is the last institution
on earth to give the people something for nothing! The fees of the
confessional show the opposite to be true, where the priest gives

nothing for something." The editor offered Fr. Noll space for a rejoinder, which he made in such a way that the pastor's ignorance was exposed, and Pastor Rose was later asked by his church's trustees to leave town.

Fr. Noll had planned a parish picnic for his first Fourth of July in Kendallville. Shortly before the day of the event, he learned that a traveling circus was to be in town but at a different location. He contacted the manager of the circus and suggested they pitch their tent on the same grounds where the picnic was to be held, since it might help increase attendance at both. The manager agreed, and during the afternoon of the big day, he came over to personally invite the young priest to come and see the show.

At the tent, the manger indicated a reserved seats area at the very top level where a flap had been opened to provide a nice breeze. Just as the young priest sat down, the two boards where he sat parted, and he fell to the bottom. Fortunately, he was not hurt, suffering only a small scratch on his head. The manager immediately had the defective seating repaired, and gamely, Fr. Noll returned to his original place. He enjoyed the show, but was teased for days about the athletic event he had performed for the circusgoers.

In 1901, the bishop asked Fr. Noll to take over the missions at Rome City, eight miles to the north, and at Albion, twelve miles to the southwest. The responsibility of looking after five different Catholic communities was a big job, which resulted in many hours spent waiting for the train. With today's automobiles, the trips the young pastor made seem simple, as the miles fly by quickly under modern wheels. In Fr. Noll's day, however, even the short trip to Albion was a two-day sojourn. Because of this, he could only offer Mass there once every three weeks, on a weekday, except in months that had a fifth Sunday. He rode the train from Kendallville to Avilla, where he had several hours to wait before the train to Albion. Fr. Noll used this time to ponder how he could get his message of truth out to the people more easily.

In spite of his busy schedule, Fr. Noll always kept his good humor. Once at Albion, he was staying overnight with the Phillips family in order to give the parishioners there a chance for confession and Mass the following day. When Mrs. Phillips called the menfolk to supper, her husband was coming up from the barn, while Fr. Noll had been strolling about outside. Father responded, "Fine, I'll be there in the shake of a dead lamb's tail!"

Mrs. Phillips then began to laugh and called to her husband, "See? It can't be a bad thing to say if even Fr. Noll says it."

As Mr. Phillips also started to laugh, too, Fr. Noll of course wanted to know what was so funny. Finally the Phillipses stopped laughing long enough to explain that Mrs. Phillips had recently used that same expression, "in the shake of a dead lamb's tail." But Mr. Phillips — not being a local man — had never heard it before, and thought it was "a terrible thing to say." At that, Fr. Noll joined in the laughter as well. He reassured Mrs. Phillips not to worry, that it certainly wasn't bad enough that she would have to confess it!

About this time, many itinerant faith healers began to preach on circuits throughout the United States. Chasing after signs and wonders, people packed tent meetings and revivals, hoping to see the results of the magical powers of these Christian "warriors." In the process, the public heard some pretty outrageous claims. According to reports, in one city the "power of God hit the platform, and the piano player fell off the bench but the piano kept on playing." In another, a 400-pound woman being prayed for fell out on the tent floor and when she got up "over 200 pounds had supernaturally disappeared from her body and all her undergarments fell to the floor."

Ever logical, Fr. Noll came to the conclusion that those healing claims that were not outright fraud must have happened by the power of suggestion. After reading a book on hypnotism and suggestion written by a priest, he decided to make a test. He called on old Mrs. Scanlan, who was in bed with the "grippe," and who told him she had a horrible headache. At once, the young priest assured her that he could cure her headache. "Oh, I know you can, Father," she replied.

He had her look at a knob on the door of her coal stove and, putting his hand on her forehead, told her that her headache would be over in a few seconds. He then assured her that it was going, going, and gone. At that, she burst out, "It *is* all gone, Father!"

From that, Fr. Noll concluded that the patient's confidence in the "healer" was the major portion of the cure. However, his test boomeranged on him. The next day, she told some of her neighbors that the priest had performed a miracle! Ruefully, he was forced to admit that the commotion that followed her comments "led me to give up even that much of a medical practice."

Fr. Noll had already, however, made a second test on the young niece of his housekeeper. After "suggesting" a cure for the cramps she had gotten after some strenuous exercise, he paid her a dime to slightly burn her finger on the stove, and cured the pain in the same manner. From this, he drew a strong conclusion:

> Many people, physically sound organically, have imaginary illnesses over which they worry. The physician can cure them with colored water, if they have implicit faith in him and in his medicine. Today, many ministers of the gospel who claim to be "faith healers" take advantage of such people. They have a large following and make a handsome living on the gullibility of those who trust them. They are not "faith" curists, but the relief their patrons receive is due almost entirely to the withdrawal of their mind from their real or imaginary ailments.

Armed with a Pen

In 1902, a storm of controversy arose in the parish of Besancon caused by the building of a Catholic school in opposition to the French parishioners' wishes. Eventually, the parish became so split over the matter that the pastor resigned.

Because of the clever way Fr. Noll had managed to transfer the priest's residence from Ligonier to Kendallville, he had already gained a reputation as a troubleshooter, and was becoming known as resourceful, diplomatic, and talented as a peacemaker. The bishop asked him to go and attempt to put out the fires of dissension at Besancon. In spite of his worry at not knowing the French language well, Fr. Noll agreed. He had been at Kendallville for four years and was much loved by the people who hated to see him leave. Two magnificent gifts he received on leaving were a rubber-tired surrey — the latest thing in transportation — and a windmill, so he wouldn't have to draw his own well water.

When he arrived at Besancon, Fr. Noll realized that the interior of the church needed repairs and redecorating, and set about trying to make it as appealing as possible with several new improvements. He believed that churches should be attractive, so in addition to the needed repairs, he also donated a beautiful side altar.

At the same time, he began trying to reconcile the half of the membership who had quit attending church. He began to visit each family, patiently listening to their catalog of complaints. After each had finished his long list of grudges, with great common sense and tact he explained that since the previous pastor was now gone, and the bishop who had ordered the school built was dead, it was senseless for them to endanger their immortal souls by continuing to stay away. His calm reasoning made sense, and slowly, the families began to return — but, still distrustful, they stayed at the back of the church.

So how would he get them to the front? Once again, the young pastor hit on a tricky solution to a thorny problem.

In those days, families occupied designated pews and, every fall, paid a "pew rent" to the church for the pew they selected. That fall, Fr. Noll appointed delegates from each part of the parish and had them meet in a committee to re-allocate the pews. During the meeting he pointed out that some pews must be better than others, so perhaps different rates should be charged. Since so many seemed to prefer the back pews, the sly young priest suggested that these pews should be charged the highest rates. The committee enthusiastically approved the plan and, when it was announced the following week, many of the former rebels paid for pews closer to the front.

Then, because he was still not completely comfortable with the language, he invited a French Jesuit to come and give a stirring mission. At the end, he was happy to see more than ninety percent of his parish receive the Sacraments for the first time in several years.

But Fr. Noll wasn't the only one in the parish with a few tricks up his sleeve. Shortly after his arrival in the parish, one of the rebellious parishioners played a joke on the young pastor. Fr. Noll had just gone to bed when he heard a pounding on his door. He opened it to see a man, obviously under the influence of alcohol, standing on his porch. At first a bit frightened, the priest was unsure of the man's intentions — but at last, the man managed to mumble that his grandmother was sick and wanted the priest. Fr. Noll had his doubts; but, in case a soul was really in need, he got his sick call kit, woke the handyman, and they all started for the outlying farm where the man lived. The man's drunken conversation on the way was humorous, and John tried to get some sense out of him, but failed.

On arrival, the man woke his mother and began yelling in French at his grandmother. Startled, the young priest looked to the mother for an explanation. Hastily she told him that the nearly 90-year-old woman was stone deaf and French was the only language she understood. Excited by being awakened from a sound sleep, the old woman didn't believe Fr. Noll was really a priest. As she didn't seem sick at all, Fr. Noll simply bid the family good night, thinking he could return another day if needed. It was only later that he learned that the man had played a trick on him. The Frenchman had been drinking with a buddy and made a bet that he could find "some sucker" to drive him the sixteen miles home.

Another time, the young priest decided to teach "by example." He took to walking about the parish grounds while saying his breviary, hoping to inspire those who saw him. Unfortunately, his plan was not successful. One of his parishioners told another that he didn't "know about that young feller — all he ever does is walk around and read."

Once he had reunited the divided parish, Fr. Noll began to think of a way to help educate his people more about their faith. His brief talks on Sunday were simply not enough, and at last he hit on an idea. He wrote a little booklet that he called *Kind Words from the Priest to His People*. Although in many ways it was simply a tactful defense of his predecessor, it was also a call for unity and harmony. It was the first of its kind: *printed material written especially for the average layman, in terms he could easily understand*. The parish welcomed this little booklet with delight, as a gift from their pastor. Although he didn't realize it, one of Fr. John Noll's greatest works had begun — the apostolate of the press.

Seeing the smashing success of his work, John realized the people's hunger for truth. What was true of the average Catholic in his small parish might also be true for a wider audience. Using the *Catholic Directory*'s listing of parishes, he handwrote envelopes and mailed copies of the pamphlet, renamed *Kind Words from Your Pastor*, to priests all over the United States. Almost immediately a flood of correspondence deluged the young priest, with requests for hundreds and thousands of copies to be distributed in parishes throughout the country.

Between his assignments in Besancon and Hartford City, the bishop allowed Fr. Noll to spend a year doing parish missions. This was a popular method of reviving parishes and of speaking to Protestant audiences, and Paulist Fathers Isaac Hecker and Walter Elliot were leaders in this. So the young priest spent the year traveling through Indiana offering these missions. During this year, he also met Thomas Price and James Walsh, who later founded the Foreign Mission Society of America (Maryknoll).

And, once again, he came up with an innovative idea that helped him get the message out even more clearly. Fr. Noll began putting out a Question Box at these missions, to find out what the people wanted to know about the Church. The box was so popular that he used these questions as the basis for some of his lectures and writings.

Noll's parents at their Roche Street home in Huntington

Hartford City

In 1906, Fr. Noll was transferred to Hartford City. In the late 1800s, the area was booming and twelve glass factories operated on the inexpensive natural gas produced in the area. Large donations enabled a nice church to be built for the city and its two missions. Shortly after the turn of the century, however, the gas dried up, and with it, the industry was forced to move out of state. The pastor preached a sermon against the highly speculative efforts of some corporations to drill for new sources of natural gas, which offended one of the parishioners, and the dispute got out of hand. Once again, the peacemaker priest, Noll, was called in to restore unity.

Here, as in the cities before, he found himself explaining the Catholic position to non-Catholics and Catholics alike. In his peacemaking efforts, he relied on his personal talks and visits to his parishioners. He continued to combat anti-Catholicism with common sense, the truth, and the basic sense of fair play he believed all Americans possessed.

Hartford City was a town of many saloons. The glass workers, laboring in the heat all day, liked to relax at the end of the day with a beer. A prohibitionist movement attempted to pressure the young priest, but Fr. Noll did not intend to turn his pulpit into a propaganda mill for prohibition. Instead, he announced and gave an open lecture on "Temperance and Total Abstinence," which was well attended. Since he had interested listeners, he used the occasion to announce a series of lectures at his church on Catholic belief and practice. As with his other lectures, these had the effect of returning a few lost sheep to the flock and of adding a few new converts as well.

During his four years at Hartford City, Fr. Noll continued to expose the chicanery of the "ex-priest" speakers who came to the area to inflame the fire of anti-Catholicism. Once the frauds were exposed and were unable to profit from the normal collections, the speakers retreated from the area, and the people became more open to hearing the truth about Catholic beliefs.

Once, Fr. Noll was called to attend a sick young woman in Montpellier. Her appendix had burst and, although the doctor opened the area, peritonitis had set in and he gave the patient no hope of recovery. After hearing her confession, Fr. Noll told her to accept God's will peacefully, but although the doctor could not help her, God could. He said, "Too often, we ask Almighty God for favors, but we do not offer Him anything in return. It is easy for God to grant any favor, and His rule is not to be outdone in generosity. If we earnestly desire to get what we ask, we should be just as ready to give."

Fr. Noll suggested that the girl ask her parents to promise that, if she were cured, her father would return to his faith and her mother would become a Catholic. Perhaps God would perform a miracle.

The following day, Fr. Noll came from Hartford City to say Mass at the mission. After Mass, the girl's brother came up to him and invited him to come to their house for dinner. Saying that he should probably wait, since the girl was so sick, the boy smilingly replied that it was his sister who had issued the invitation. On arrival, the patient informed him that she was going to recover but that she knew it was God's work, not the doctor's. She told him her parents had promised what she had asked them, and expressed her confidence in her complete recovery.

Some time later Fr. Noll met the girl's doctor on the interurban.[3] "I don't understand Miss Kerwin's recovery," the doctor said. "She didn't have one chance in a million to recover at all, yet alone so rapidly!"

Many of the families in Hartford City were poor. One of the children set to make First Communion was sad, as her family could not afford the trappings for the big day. Fr. Noll bought some soap and gave it to the little girl to sell. With the proceeds, she was able to purchase what she needed. By giving her the soap instead of just handing her the needed money, Fr. Noll allowed her to keep her pride. The following day was a school holiday for the children, and Fr. Noll took the entire class to the amusement park as a treat. They rode everything rideable, ate everything edible and not so edible, and had a glorious time.

In 1910, Fr. Noll was transferred to St. Mary's in Huntington. The entire parish at Hartford City gathered to give the young pastor a fond farewell. Little Leo Pursley, a second grader, was chosen to stand and recite a farewell speech, which the young boy always remembered. Years later, Fr. Pursley was chosen the sixth Bishop of Fort Wayne, becoming Archbishop John Noll's successor as head of the diocese.

CHAPTER SEVEN

THE FIRST PRINT SHOP

Fr. Noll always remained concerned with combating prejudice against the Church. At this time in the history of the United States, the great waves of immigrants, many of whom were Catholic, had incited a xenophobic reaction in many native Americans. In particular, many Americans saw the Catholic Church as "foreign."

To counter this, Fr. Noll saw the great importance of a well-informed laity. Long before the directives of the Second Vatican Council, or the move for Catholic Action, he realized that the laity had a special mission of education:

> Many people who are literally steeped in prejudice would become disposed to embrace the Catholic Faith if they were approached with charity and kindness, and if the Catholic Church were given a chance to speak for itself. Unfortunately, the priest does not meet so many non-Catholics as does the layman, and that is why every Catholic should be an apostle, representing his Church creditably before his neighbors and the people among who he works. If it becomes known that he is earnest, derives great joy from his Faith, and that his ideals are outstandingly higher than those of others, people must be attracted, even insensibly, to the religion that stands for those ideals.

Studying how to achieve a better-informed laity — since the average Catholic would hardly be inclined to read voluminous tomes of theology — Fr. Noll hit on the idea of periodical literature. He received an excellent little 32-page monthly magazine called *Truth*, put out by Fr. Thomas F. Price.[4] Fr. Noll hit on the idea of taking off the cover, adding four or eight pages of local parish news and a new cover, and calling it *The Parish Monthly*. He wrote to Fr. Price, telling him not to bother covering the issues for his parish; on hearing what Fr. Noll was doing, Fr. Price sent letters to the other American clergy encouraging them to adopt Noll's idea.

By the end of the first year, Fr. Noll discovered his own talent for writing and began producing the magazine himself. Some neighboring pastors asked for copies and the circulation began to grow. Fr. Noll then sent copies to the pastors of large parishes throughout the country, explaining his system and suggesting they could sell local advertisements to bring in enough revenue to support the production. Soon, more than 50 parishes were subscribing to the center core of this magazine, adding their own material and cover. Most of the subscribing parishes, however, preferred Fr. Noll to handle the printing of the entire magazine. As circulation grew, the printers in Hartford City could no longer keep up with it, so much of the printing was moved to a large firm in Muncie. Fr. Noll somehow oversaw all this in addition to keeping up with his duties as pastor of a lively church and mission.

By 1910, Fr. Noll had begun to receive national recognition as a Catholic publicist. In order to allow him more time for his writing and editing efforts, Bishop Alerding appointed him pastor of St. Mary's parish in Huntington, giving him an assistant to share the work. A local printer offered to sell Noll a nearby state-of-the-art print shop he no longer needed. The man had leased property from the parish to establish the shop, thinking to found a second paper for the city. Realizing that only one paper could be profitable in the little town, he bought out the existing paper and offered Fr. Noll a deep discount on the new shop. Fr. Noll bought the shop and hired a team to print *The Parish Monthly*.[5]

Our Sunday Visitor

Between 1909 and 1912, a virulent form of socialism came to America. It was opposed to religion, morality, and private ownership. Around 1911, one Socialist organization began to publish *The Menace*, a periodical devoted to propaganda against religion in general and the Catholic Church in particular.[6] The paper became a veritable cash cow for its promoters, and many imitators sprang up. Then, as today with many other forms of hate literature, people were often introduced to *The Menace* by receiving a copy of it on their front porch, left clandestinely. A wave of bigotry began to lash the country. The tricky charlatans who toured the country gave enormously profitable lectures. Often speaking under the auspices of some gullible Protestant congregation who fell for the Socialist line of "equality for all," the speakers took up collections and promoted subscriptions to their inflammatory papers.

The Catholic Church had no organized defense against these attacks, so Fr. Noll decided that a weekly publication was needed to defend the Church and to provide catechesis for the adult laity. He had his printers copy a few pages of *The Menace* and mailed it to priests throughout the country with a letter asking if they would support the publication of a national Catholic paper to combat it. The paper, costing 1 cent per issue, would be delivered to the parish to be distributed free to the congregation on Sunday morning.

On May 5, 1912, the first issues of the new paper named *Our Sunday Visitor* rolled off the presses in Huntington and began to spread throughout the United States with an initial press run of 35,000.

First issue of *Our Sunday Visitor,* 1912   From a 1915 issue of *Our Sunday Visitor*

At its peak in 1961, the paper reached a million copies in circulation and Our Sunday Visitor, Inc. became one of the world's largest Catholic publishers. Although today diocesan newspapers have taken over much of the work of *Our Sunday Visitor,* the publication remains the largest national Catholic weekly. (Fr. Noll soon brought in Francis A. Fink, a Notre Dame graduate, as managing editor of *Our Sunday Visitor,* a move that greatly helped him as his responsibilities increased.)

In the 1920s, Fr. Noll sold lifetime subscriptions to raise additional funds for the paper. These subscriptions cost $100. At the time, that was an almost unheard-of sum to be asking for such a thing, since it was the equivalent of about $5,000 today, but many people still responded favorably.

One of his parishioners at St. Mary's, Jacob "Jake" Young, purchased a subscription in his son Jay's name. Young Jay was stationed in Washington, D.C., in 1944, when the U.S. bishops held

Staff photo, 1914. Fr. Noll is back row, left

their annual conference there. Learning where Bishop Noll was staying, Jay gave him a call. As a former parishioner, he wanted to extend his good wishes. The young Navy ensign was delighted when the Bishop not only remembered him, but also asked about his parents and their health.

Meanwhile, Fr. Noll's crusade against the hate-mongers continued.

Since many of the speakers still pretended to be ex-priests or ex-nuns, he wrote a letter to all of the Catholic bishops in the U.S. suggesting they send a representative to the advertised speeches who would stand up and ask the purported priest where he was ordained, or what religious order he or she belonged to. He personally gathered reliable information on more than 100 of these fakes and published it in a booklet entitled *Defamers of the Church*. When he also publicized the background of the publishers of *The Menace*, many people became ashamed that

Cover of an anti-Catholic book published in Noll's time and still published today

An early staff picnic at Noll Hill

they had supported the paper and angry that they had been taken in. And finally, since most of the speakers on the lucrative anti-Catholic circuit relied on a standard stock set of charges against the church, so Fr. Noll published a poster with a number of these false charges and sent it out with the offer of a $1,000 reward to anyone who could prove a single one of the charges was true. The reward was never claimed.

With the growth in circulation of the paper, there came a deluge of mail. Fr. Noll made it a personal rule to answer each letter that came to the paper. As long as he remained at the paper, he handled this chore himself.

As circulation of his Catholic publications grew, Fr. Noll's publishing operation began doing contract publishing for other groups. He retained the ownership until he liquidated the debt incurred in purchasing the equipment; then, in 1915, he formed a corporation under the Indiana charitable laws. Thereafter, all profits were distributed by Our Sunday Visitor to support various Catholic causes. In 1976, this system of organized giving became Our Sunday Visitor Institute, which still distributes millions of dollars annually to Catholic endeavors.

An excellent businessman, Fr. Noll ran the printing business very profitably. For him, though, it was never "his" money; all that he had belonged in the service of the Church.

In spite of the tremendous amount of charitable work Fr. Noll was able to do, often using his own personal funds, during the last two years of his life he often worried that he had not been charitable enough. Disabled by a stroke, he had much time for thought and reflection, and mentioned this worry to several close friends who visited him. Those who know his record in this regard, or who felt the effects of his personal charitable efforts, know that he had nothing to worry about on this score.

Church Envelopes

In 1916, most Catholic parishes were funded by pew rents as well as weekly and monthly collections. Always quick to adapt good ideas to his own situation, Fr. Noll read a press release from the National Council of the Churches of Christ in America that advocated giving member families a box of envelopes for their weekly donations to support both the church and the missions. This would elicit funds from even non-practicing members. He experimented with the idea in his own parish, dropping pew rents and the monthly collection, and distributing the envelopes to each family. He was surprised to discover that his parish received more than double their usual amount of money this way. Soon a new division was added to his busy presses, and today, the OSV offering envelope division is the largest of its kind in the world.

Fr. Noll was used to hard work; sixteen-hour workdays weren't uncommon for him. This was how he could put forth enormous efforts in the publishing field without disrupting any of his duties as pastor of a thriving parish. Daily, he taught catechism at the parish school, and he personally instructed most of the converts. In addition, he conducted popular lectures on the Faith that were always open to Catholics and non-Catholics alike.

In addition to the normal chores of a parish priest, Fr. Noll was faced with a number of repairs to the parish property, including arranging for a different type of heating system. His care for the city didn't end at parish boundaries, either. Amid all his other heavy work, he was quick to lend his efforts to the promotion of the general welfare of the city. At heart, Fr. Noll was a peace-maker, and he valued harmony so much that he subtitled his newspaper "The Harmonizer," putting those words directly under the newspaper's title banner.

When the Rotary club came to Huntington, Fr. Noll became a charter member. Unlike many other social and professional clubs, Rotary held their meetings at lunchtime, so the pastor didn't feel as if he was taking any time away from his priestly concerns. Fr. Noll's nametag read simply "Jack Noll" — since title and position are not essential in Rotary — and his membership gave him a chance to become better acquainted with the business and profes-sional men of the city. They, in their turn, had rarely had the oppor-tunity to be around a Catholic priest. Their acquaintance with Fr. Noll, who was always open and willing to answer their questions, resulted in their understanding Catholics much better.

When the Ku Klux Klan came to Huntington, a group of Fr. Noll's Rotary friends came to him and pledged that not one of their members would join the group and all would attempt to show it for the hate-mongering organization it really was. For his part, of course, Father did all he could to expose the Klan.

As the success of Fr. Noll's publications became known, more Catholic publications around the country sprang up. In 1911, Fr. Noll helped found the Catholic Press Association.

Because of the rapid growth of the newspaper and the other publications, a larger headquarters was built for the publishing house in 1924. In 1925, understanding that priests themselves needed quality popular literature, covering subjects that would interest them alone, Fr. Noll began another monthly magazine called *The Acolyte*. The original name was chosen to give the idea that the magazine would help the priest just as an acolyte, or altar server, assists him at Mass. Eventually, at Fr. Noll's suggestion, the magazine was "ordained" and re-named *The Priest*.

Good Catholic Books

In addition to periodicals, Fr. Noll also began to write and publish books and pamphlets[7] generally devoted to teaching the faith. Recognizing there was often a need for short articles to clarify some phase of Catholic doctrine, he began to produce a flood of these short, easily read, and popular pamphlets pastors could distribute from racks in church foyers.

Gifted with a phenomenal memory, Fr. Noll read quickly and was an inveterate clipper of anything he thought he might need or use later. Of course, this led to a somewhat messy work area and, more than once, an amusing incident. Piles of clippings and notes cluttered his desk. When the bookshelves were filled, books landed on chairs, a small table, and even the floor. Father's office was the despair of anyone with a bent for tidiness. People who visited were invariably amazed when the Bishop would mention an article from months previously — then immediately reach for, and retrieve, it from the correct stack.

Once, a Huntington police patrolman was passing by the Visitor building and noticed an open door. Cautiously he called for backup, keeping the door in sight, and on the other officer's arrival, they began to search the building. All seemed fine until they reached the bishop's office. Immediately, they were certain it had been searched and burglarized. One officer phoned the bishop's home to have the prelate come down and identify what had been stolen.

Father's secretary and assistant (his niece, Cecilia Fink) answered the call. When the officer informed her there had been a burglary, she was immediately concerned.

"Oh, dear! What happened?" she said in alarm.

The officer explained that a door to the Visitor building had been found open and, when police searched the building, they saw that Fr. Noll's office had apparently been burglarized, since it looked like a whirlwind had hit it. Hearing this, Cecilia burst out in peals of laughter.

"Don't worry," she gasped out. "His office is always like that!"

One of the first copies of *Father Smith Instructs Jackson*

Fr. Noll's first book was intended to help explain the Faith to interested non-Catholics. He used the novel concept of quoting Protestant sources to defend the Catholic Faith. Published in 1914, it was originally titled *For Our Non-Catholic Friends,* but succeeding editions were re-named as *The Fairest Argument.* Over 500 Protestant sources were quoted in the book.

Noll's best-known book is *Father Smith Instructs Jackson*, published in 1913, which presented doctrinal instruction in dialogue style. Originally published in the newspaper as a series of conferences between "Father Smith" and a catechumen named "Jones," each article was a conference between the two characters. The series proved immensely popular, which led to its being published in book form. Widely circulated, the book remains in print today.

Fr. Noll studied the methods of the opposition forces and often turned things to his own use. He noticed the popularity of a little book called *A Socialist Vest-Pocket Book of Facts.* Soon he produced a little book, of the same size and portability, which he titled *A Vest Pocket Book of Catholic Facts.* It was a convenient format that a man could take with him in his vest pocket, or a lady could easily stash in her purse, then have the reference at hand when needed. The book became an immediate best seller, and remained so through several revisions, until after World War II.

As prolific a writer as he was, Fr. Noll recognized the need for good Catholic books — written in a contemporary, readable style — by other authors. By the early 1920s, he began to publish works by other Catholic authors who shared his vision of educating the laity through the use of modern media.[8] Today, Our Sunday Visitor Books is one of the largest and best-known Catholic publishing houses in the world. It offers over 500 products for sale through parishes, bookstores, and the Internet.

The Journalist

Fr. Noll's was the heart, soul, and pen of a journalist, not a literary writer bent on entertaining or creating art. His was a mission to teach, writing for his day and in a simple style that everyone could understand. No one needed a degree in theology or a dictionary to read the books and articles written and initialed by J.F.N., or Lon Francis, as he was also called. Pen names were popular in Fr. Noll's day and, in selecting one for his occasional use, he took the simple expedient of reversing his name. If sometimes his editorial comments were not exact, he simply smiled and said, "Day after tomorrow, no one will remember what I wrote anyway."

The busy journalist's desk was never orderly; photo, 1922

A fluent writer even when his own hand held the pen, as he aged, Fr. Noll began to dictate many things in order to be able to produce even more. By his late forties, he could dictate a 10,000-word article, replete with references, in twenty minutes. His mind was like a sponge, retaining many of the references he needed;

otherwise, he could walk to his horribly messy desk and pull out the exact piece of paper he wanted immediately.

Faced with the lack of a high school textbook that related religious instruction to action, he dictated a four-volume set of books that ran to over a thousand pages — in only six weeks! It took two secretaries to keep up with the rapid pace of his dictation on this project. Each new letter that landed on his desk was answered by the end of the day.

There is no exact count of the books, articles, and pamphlets he wrote. One of his pen names is known, but he may have used others. In his time, Bishop Noll was to the printed word what Bishop Fulton Sheen was to the spoken one; to this day, he remains the most outstanding Catholic publisher America has ever known.

CHAPTER EIGHT

NEVER STOP LEARNING

By 1919, Fr. Noll's exhausting schedule had caused his doctors to suggest he take a rest. At about this time, Fr. George Hickey wrote to him, saying that he planned a trip to visit South America; would Fr. Noll know anyone who would like to go along as a traveling companion? With his doctor's advice fresh in mind, Fr. Noll suggested himself.

So from January to May of 1920, Fr. Noll and Fr. Hickey toured the countries of South America, visiting all the typical tourist sights and enjoying themselves immensely. Fr. Noll took with him, however, a set of printed questions he asked each of the church officials he visited with. The questions covered religious, economic, social, and educational conditions in the country. The information gathered this way was good because it came from men who knew their country and what the people wanted and did not want. It was far more reliable than the information gathered by the state department from partisan politicians in these same countries.

As the publishing business grew, Fr. Noll's name became familiar throughout the country, and honors and awards began to flow in his direction. In 1915, he was awarded an honorary doctorate degree from Notre Dame, and in 1921 the Holy See elevated him to the rank of Domestic Prelate — Monsignor. At heart, though, he still thought of himself as a simple parish priest and remained in close and loving contact with friends and family.

In June of 1923, St. Mary's celebrated Msgr. Noll's Silver Jubilee. One of a number of presents presented to him on this occasion was the first radio to come to Huntington, Indiana. He took great delight in the gift. Although there were not many stations, one from Chicago came in clearly. In order to share his gift with his neighbors, Fr. Noll opened the windows in his front room and with the aid of a megaphone attachment let the music peal out through the neighborhood.

An early radio

The Visitor's gift to the Jubilarian was the offer of an extended trip to Europe for him and a companion. In January of 1924, he and his cousin, Fr. Raymond Noll, traveled to New York, where they expected to embark by ship for Europe. Arriving in the city, they discovered that their original ship had problems and would not be able to sail on time. Remembering that a Mr. Lilly, a good friend of the Visitor, was in the shipping business, Fr. John Noll contacted him to see if other arrangements could be made. He was surprised to hear back from the man that indeed he could put them on a ship the following day — that is, provided they could obtain the necessary visas by the next morning.

In New York City

The Nolls were staying with their friend Msgr. Evers, who happened to be the chaplain for the city police. He had a police car and driver at his disposal. Within the next few hours, sometimes with the aid of the siren, the two priests flew through the streets of New York, visiting the consulates of all twenty countries they planned to visit.

Just as he had done when visiting South America, Fr. Noll visited all the familiar tourist sites, with special trips to warm any Catholic's heart.

He and his cousin visited many of the sacred places in the Holy Land, said Mass at the grotto at Lourdes, visited the Little Flower's grave at Lisieux, and even had a personal audience with Pope Pius XI. As soon as Fr. Noll entered the room, the Pope asked him "How is Our Sunday Visitor getting along?" It was on this trip that Fr. Noll had his first airplane ride, from Paris to London.

At the ruins of the temple at Capharnum

On the River Jordan

On board the *Conte Verbe* while anchored off Madeiva, January 1924

When Frs. John and Raymond boarded the train for Vienna, in typically American fashion, Fr. John Noll made himself comfortable, slouching back and propping his feet on the opposite bench. As the conductor passed by their compartment, he noticed Father's position and ordered the priest to put his feet on the floor immediately. He then called a policeman, who informed Fr. John Noll that he must pay a fine of 10,000 crowns for breaking the law. Alarmed at first, Fr. Noll relaxed only after he'd rapidly calculated the exchange rate and figured out that the "massive" fine was the American equivalent of fifteen cents.

Once again, just as he had in South America, Fr. Noll kept asking questions. Every place in Europe was in a state of unrest and no government seemed secure. He saw for himself the threat of Communism.

Far more alarming than the "infamous" fine Fr. Noll received for propping his feet on the train were the reports of his German informants. Fr. Noll reported:

> The antics of the mark in 1924 were enough to drive the people mad. There was no incentive to work, much less

to save. . . . The political agitations have done much to divide the people of Germany, and there as in any country, it is a case of "divided we fall." The Bavarians who, left to themselves, would be quite placid and religious, have been stirred up by Hitler and Ludendorf. Ludendorf, the Prussian, the anti-Catholic unwelcome in his own home, has moved into the heart of Bavaria, which is Catholic, and there has launched a bitter attack against the

In Egypt near the Sphinx

Standing in the Nile River

Catholic Church and her Cardinal at their very door. In an anti-Catholic campaign, Ludendorf and Hitler are united, though they are otherwise promoters of different programs.

He went on to compare Hitler's program to the Ku Klux Klan.

CHAPTER NINE

A NATIONAL BISHOP

Bishop Alerding died in December of 1924; on May 13, 1925, Fr. Noll was formally notified that he had been selected by Pope Pius XI to fill the vacant see at Fort Wayne.

The consecration was set for June 30, the feast of St. Paul. The only other bishop from Indiana was asked to preach the sermon, but the day before the consecration, he sent word that he was too ill even to attend. At this last moment, who could be asked to pinch hit? Only one man seemed suitable: the elderly Msgr. Cleary of Minneapolis, a noted Chautauqua lecturer.[9]

At about 11 P.M. on the night before the ceremony, the elderly Monsignor was sleeping soundly when a powerful rapping at his hotel door awoke him. (Shortly before, the jangling of his telephone had failed to rouse him.) Sleepily, he called out, "Who's there?"

Pope Pius XI elevated Noll to the Bishopric

Frantically, the bishop-elect answered, "It's me — John Noll, the person you came here to honor."

There was a moment's silence before the old priest replied, "Go to bed. You're drunk!"

"No, no, only open the door," Fr. Noll said, fearful that the entire floor might be awakened. "I really need to talk to you."

Bishop Alerding, left, Noll's predecessor, at the cabin on Bishop's Island

Cautiously the door opened a few inches while the elderly priest sized up the situation. Seeing that Fr. Noll certainly seemed sober, if extremely worried, he invited the younger man in. As soon as Fr. Noll made his plea for help, Msgr. Cleary sent him home, telling him to get some rest, and that he (Msgr. Cleary) would do the worrying about the sermon. The following day, he preached an eloquent and impassioned sermon on the office of a bishop.

Bishop Noll, c. 1951

In choosing the motto for his coat of arms, *Mentes Tuorum Visita*, Noll picked a phrase from an ancient hymn of the Church that invokes the Holy Spirit to visit, to come and dwell, with His divine truth, in the minds of men. Impelled by apostolic zeal, he translated his motto into action.

Because of his experience with national and international issues, Bishop Noll immediately became an influential leader among U.S. prelates. He was named secretary of

The new Bishop

Bishop Noll with pages at his consecration

Outside the Cathedral of the Immaculate Conception on the big day. Bishop Noll's father is in the second row, just behind the late George Cardinal Mundelein of Chicago (first row, third from right), who presided at the consecration.

the fledgling National Catholic Welfare Conference (now the United States Conference of Catholic Bishops), and was a long-time member of that body's administrative committee. In his role with the bishops' conference, Bishop Noll again demonstrated his foresight about the coming information age, helping to launch the Catholic News Service and the *Catholic Hour* on NBC radio.

In spite of his tremendous workload — which doubled with the responsibilities of his elevation — Bishop Noll remained a warm and loving person, a man in love with his God, his Church, and his family. His personal style had always been, and remained, easygoing and informal. Those who knew him considered him comfortable and "homey" with a delicious sense of humor.

A Finger in Every Pie

Once elevated to the episcopacy, it seemed, Fr. Noll had a finger in every Catholic pie in the country. He lived during a time of momentous change in the world, and during his 31 years as bishop, he became one of the leading figures of the Catholic Church in the United States. A staunch defender of the Church, he saw the need for her presence on the national level. He would prove to the world that a man could be both Catholic and American.

After an audience with the Pope in 1929

A visionary and a man consistently ahead of his time, the Bishop recognized the need for Catholic action on the part of the laity and implemented many programs in this regard. In 1937, he charged the graduates of St. Mary's College of Notre Dame:

> The Church of God must depend upon her laity, who associate daily with the general populace, to infiltrate society with the right principals of morality. The Church, through its spiritual leaders, calls on you to participate in such an Apostolate, appropriately called Catholic Action. Will you respond?

Bishop Noll visited Europe three more times before the war years. In 1929, he made his first *Ad Limina* visit to Rome, and continued traveling with a group on a Catholic tour to a number of other countries.

In 1930, he was asked by a group of Hungarian Americans to accompany them as their chaplain on a tour to celebrate the ninth centenary of the death of St. Emeric, son of St. Stephen, patron of Hungary. A high point of this trip for Fr. Noll was the opportunity to have an extended visit with the German stigmatic, Theresa Neumann, and a chance to observe her in ecstasy.

Theresa Neumann, the German mystic, whose Cause for Beatification is currently active (left)

Theresa Neumann as she looked at the time when she received the stigmata (right)

In 1938, he made a second visit to Rome. As always, he questioned and learned. The knowledge he gained helped him speak out and write about the world, and he soon became one of the best-informed priests in the United States.

Bishop Noll wrote and publicized information on the problems in Mexico in the 1920s and 30s, as he did shortly after the Spanish Civil War. Because of our economic interests in the country, the American government was hesitant to do anything about the drastic situation in the country next door. Bishop Noll and *Our Sunday Visitor* joined the Knights of Columbus and the Extension Society in working to show the American public the atrocities of the persecution of the Church in Mexico.

MEXICO'S PERSECUTION OF THE CHURCH

CALLES, THE PERSECUTOR

Friends of Catholic Mexico booklet: *Calles, the Persecutor*

Noll appointed Robert Hull to study and publicize the plight of the afflicted people of Mexico and established a group known as The Friends of Catholic Mexico to work for this goal. As a member of the administrative committee of the NCWC, he helped to draft the

The execution of Bl. Miguel Pro, S.J., one of many priests killed in Mexico

The body of Bl. Anacleto Gonzalez Flores, tortured and murdered for his faith; with his widow and children

written position of the American Hierarchy, which pushed the President of the United States for action to settle the Cristero War.

Extremely concerned about the way the Church was being treated by anti-Catholic forces in Europe as well, Bishop Noll wrote and warned of the problems brewing there, and the menace of Communism. He was an inveterate foe of this ideology. Just like many Catholic journalists after him, Fr. Noll found that the secular press was not always reliable and that, even with the best of intentions, it often printed an erroneous picture of the real status of affairs in a foreign country. As he said:

> Most emissaries of our government to those countries visited none other than the politicians. It was usually announced in the papers that the gentleman was coming to their country, so he would be met at the boat by representatives of the government in power and seldom got out of their hands. Naturally, this resulted in a report to the press that was in favor of the government in power. I believe that the information I gathered has been very helpful in correcting erroneous ideas spread through the columns of the American press.

Bishop Noll found the Europe of the 1920s in the state of unrest that eventually culminated in the Second World War. Fascism was rampant in Italy, Communism was completing its conquest of Russia, and Hitler was beginning his evil works in Germany. He told the readers of *Our Sunday Visitor*, "In those countries which participated most actively in the war (World War I), the poor have become destitute [and] the middle classes poor, while the rich, in many instances, have grown richer."

The Sisters

Bishop Noll's first public act after he became Bishop was the dedication of the new motherhouse for the Missionary Sisters of Our Lady of Victory.

Victory Noll, the motherhouse in Huntington

In 1920, Bishop Noll was serving on the board of the Catholic Extension Society, a group dedicated to supporting mission churches in this country. In parts of the United States, there were few Catholics. Often, there was no nearby parish, and many children had no opportunity for even the basics of education in the Faith. In 1905, Fr. Francis Clement Kelley had organized the Extension Society to foster and extend the faith in these areas. Both Fr. Noll and Fr. Kelly were whirlwinds of apostolic zeal, and the two men became close friends. Later, Archbishop William O'Brien headed the group, and he and Bishop Noll also became close friends and allies. Almost from the beginning, Bishop Noll had been an enthusiastic promoter of *Extension*. He was able to use the immense circulation of the newspaper to garner funds, religious items, and even personnel for the missions.

Fr. Kelly asked Bishop Noll to establish a home mission seminary near Huntington to prepare priests for the mission territories in the Western United States. Enthusiastically, Fr. Noll purchased a large farm just west of Huntington for this purpose. The Western bishops, however, had different ideas. They believed they could encourage local vocations in their own areas, men and women who would be familiar with the people and their customs, so the Bishops asked Our Sunday Visitor to help fund these boys' seminary studies. Thus, the Huntington seminary project was set aside.

A few years later, a wealthy man from California named Peter O'Donnell called on Bishop Noll after Mass one day in Hot Springs, Arkansas, while both were taking a brief vacation to enjoy the much-touted mineral baths. They were equally delighted to meet in person, as they had been in contact via correspondence for some time. O'Donnell was a former police sergeant from Chicago who had retired to the Los Angeles area. He and his wife had invested in some land that they later discovered was often under water. Fearing that they had made a poor investment and would lose their money, they asked the Blessed Mother's help and promised to give half of any profit to a worthy charity. Shortly thereafter, they were able to sell the land for ten times what they had paid for it.

In traveling through southern California, O'Donnell was horrified to discover that thousands of Mexican children received no form of religious education. There were over 150,000 of them in the city of Los Angeles alone, and many more were scattered throughout the southern part of the state. He had asked help from his local bishop, but no personnel were available to be dedicated to that type of work. Discouraged not to be able to keep his promise to Our Lady, he begged Bishop Noll to begin a group of religious women who would work as missionary catechists in the Southwest. If the Bishop could begin such a group, establishing a motherhouse for them in Huntington, O'Donnell promised to give him $50,000 for the purpose.

Bishop Noll told O'Donnell that although he empathized with his wish, he was so committed that he did not think he could do justice to the idea of forming a new group. "However," he continued, "I know of a group in Chicago that might fit the bill." But O'Donnell insisted that the motherhouse should be in Huntington, feeling that Fr. Noll would give it better attention than if it were in Chicago.

The two men parted on the agreement that Fr. Noll would visit the Chicago group to check out the possibility of their coming to Indiana. What neither man suspected was how God was already working to make the plan a reality.

In 1915, a frail young hospital chaplain in Chicago, Fr. John Sigstein, had begun a group of men and women to aid the missions. Called the Society of Missionary Helpers of Our Blessed Lady of Victory, the members collected discarded church goods and vestments and repaired or refurbished them for the missions. From them, he recruited the first two members of a Society of Missionary Catechists, a sisterhood to fulfill his dream of instructing poor Mexican children in the Southwest. In 1922, these first sisters began working in the Archdiocese of Santa Fe.

Bishop Noll visited with Fr. Sigstein, outlining O'Donnell's plan. As the postulants for the fledgling community were living with the School sisters of Notre Dame, Fr. Sigstein was delighted with the idea. He readily agreed to the move, if his bishop would agree. The next thing both of them knew, Cardinal Mundelein released Sigstein to the Diocese of Fort Wayne, and Fr. Noll began to build a beautiful Spanish-style motherhouse on the land he had originally bought for a mission seminary.

The bishop then began to beat the drums enthusiastically for these catechists, through the *Our Sunday Visitor* newspaper; by the time the motherhouse was habitable, nearly a dozen young women were eager to move in.

So, on December 7, 1924, Fr. Sigstein, nine catechists, and a probationer (postulant) arrived on the train from Gary, Indiana. Although the building was far from complete, it was livable enough, and the sisters were thrilled to have their own home. After supper, Bishop Noll, along with Fr. Kelly and a man named Clarence Dougherty, came out to visit the sisters. This was a fortunate visit; the trucks carrying the sisters' household goods and bedding had not yet arrived, but Bishop Noll came to the rescue — he and Clarence

With a group of Victory Noll novices in 1944

simply went over to his family's summer cottage, not far from the motherhouse, to get bedding and a few other items the sisters needed.

Fr. Sigstein decided to call the motherhouse Victory Noll, in honor of both Our Lady and the priest who was to become their greatest benefactor. As the property sat on a hill overlooking the Wabash River, Fr. Sigstein especially liked the way the name "Noll" lent itself to a play on words, calling to mind the word "knoll." Although Bishop Noll wasn't consulted about the name beforehand, it was obvious from his broad smile on hearing the new name that he was pleased.

Fr. Noll publicized the work of the catechists through *Our Sunday Visitor*, and published a weekly column in which one of the catechists detailed their work of visiting homes, locating children in need of religious instruction, even starting new parishes. More than one of the sisters claimed they realized their vocation through Bishop Noll and the *Sunday Visitor*.

As a senior student at Ohio University, Carmela Farley was the only Catholic living in her co-op housing. As such, the other roomers often asked her questions about the faith. When she didn't know the answer, she told them, "I'll find out." She wrote her questions to *Our Sunday Visitor*, and Noll answered her letters. Later, she credited his letters, in response to her questions, as one of the main things that motivated her vocation. She was thrilled to make her first profession to the kind bishop who had so patiently answered her. As she knelt to kiss his ring, she tripped on her skirt and fell into his lap. Instead of making a big production of the accident, he gave her a fatherly pat and helped her gently to her feet.

The society grew and received canonical recognition as a religious institute in 1932, changing their name to Missionary Sisters of Our Lady of Victory to reflect their status as a full religious institute in the church. The Missionary Catechists were a pioneering group of women who, as catechists, took a prominent role in the lives of their students, living among the people and caring for all aspects of life in mission territory.

For the rest of his life, Bishop Noll had a special place in his heart for these sisters, even choosing to be buried at their motherhouse instead of in the cathedral. (He told Sister Carmela that he figured he would get more prayers there with the sisters than

The chapel at the motherhouse

The Bishop conducts a profession ceremony at Victory Noll

he ever would in the cathedral crypt, the traditional resting place for the bishops of Fort Wayne.)

The sisters set aside a special office for Bishop Noll where he could work when he visited Victory Noll. They said they always knew when the Bishop was around, even if he tried to slip into his office quietly to get a little work done. The smoke from his cigar would rise through the vents, and the odor would give his presence away. Soon, his full-throated, hearty laughter would begin to penetrate the convent's silence.

Through the years, Bishop Noll made what he called his "annual visit" to Victory Noll. Of course, he visited at other times as well, but he rarely missed a visit each August 5, the day of reception and profession for the sisters. He conducted the services himself, and his sermon was not a formal discourse but a paternal talk.

He always displayed a loving interest in each of the sisters, whether she was a superior or a novice. Kindness and humor were hallmarks of his dealings with them: when one sister was sick on a Friday, he released her from the normal fast and abstinence restrictions to help her recover faster.

Even mistakes were passed over lightly by the Bishop, and usually treated with humor. As a novice, Sister Charlene was thrilled to be able to serve as assistant sacristan and prepare the sacred vessels and vestments for the Bishop. She carefully filled the cruets with water and wine and put them in the refrigerator until morning. But at the Offertory, she was puzzled to notice the Bishop put the drops of water in the chalice from his large pitcher. After Mass, she stopped at the credence table as she went up to blow out the candles and, to her horror, discovered that the water in the cruet had frozen, and the cruet had broken in half after she put it on the table.

As the bell rang for breakfast, she had to enter the sacristy to turn off the chapel lights. The Bishop was sitting quietly reading his breviary. Hoping he wouldn't notice her, she silently reached for the lights. But then he spoke up, wishing her a good morning. After she knelt and kissed his ring, she was going to slip away, but she wasn't quick enough to escape before he asked, "What did you do to my cruets?"

Sheepishly, she hung her head and confessed, "I froze them, Bishop."

Instead of the expected reprimand, Bishop Noll responded with hearty laughter. Then he told her to kneel and gave her his blessing.

Since their work obliged them to travel long distances, all of the sisters learned to be good drivers. Bishop Noll had never learned how to operate a car, so a number of the sisters eventually became "official drivers" for their beloved Bishop. The sisters often did double duty, pitching in as housekeepers and cooks at his home, while also serving as social workers in Fort Wayne.

Missions

Bishop Noll was a member of the Board of Catholic Missions for more than 25 years, and served as their treasurer for most of those years. Throughout his episcopate, he did much to support the missions, both those in the U.S. and also those in foreign countries.

The power of the press was clearly shown in the amount of funds received through the mission appeals in *Our Sunday Visitor.*

National Catholic Welfare Conference

At the beginning of World War I, under the influence of Cardinal James Gibbons and the direction of Msgr. John J. Burke, a National Catholic War Council, made up of all the bishops of the United States, was established to consolidate the contribution of American Catholics to the war effort. After the war, the council was renamed, and the W stood instead for "welfare." The official voluntary agency of the American bishops, its aim was to facili-

Noll with friends c. 1930s

tate discussions of policies affecting the interests and activities of the Church in the United States. (Today, its work is carried on through the U.S.C.C.B. [10)]

The Midwest bishops, who saw the need to consolidate a national presence for the Church, enthusiastically supported the NCWC. Bishop Noll's efforts in this area is one reason why he was so supportive of any national organization that would bring the power of the Church into political, social, or religious reform. Many on the NCWC would later say, "Let Noll do it," as a sign of their confidence in his ability to raise funds and organize for national causes such as the National Shrine.

Bishop Noll strolled into his first meeting of the NCWC in 1925, but no sooner was he seated than he noticed Cardinal O'Connell of Boston signaling him to come to the rostrum. Knowing the new bishop's prolific journalistic output, he whispered to Noll, "Sit here, we need you to be the secretary." (Although the Bishop "sat there" for the majority of the remainder of his episcopacy, he eventually asked for an assistant because, in spite of what the Cardinal thought, he was not skilled in shorthand!)

At that same first meeting, Bishop Noll was elected treasurer of the American Board of Catholic Missions, organized for the home missions (to tie in with the Propagation of the Faith, which aids foreign missions). With this group, also, Noll remained active for the remainder of his life.

Through the years, Bishop Noll was as active with the NCWC as he was in all other phases of his life. He served as Episcopal Chairman of Lay Organizations, sought ways to extend Catholic youth organizations, was instrumental in the early Catholic programming for radio, and successfully pushed for a national Catholic information bureau to combat what he saw as the most dangerous enemy of the Church — ignorance. He was a charter member of the Bishop's Committee on Motion Pictures, which launched the Legion of Decency, and was chairman of the committee that founded the National Organization for Decent Literature. After World War II, he was particularly touched by the plight of the many in Europe, whose homes and livelihood had been destroyed. Many of them could not go home because they had no home to go to. Bishop Noll was especially active in the work to help resettle the flood of displaced persons who immigrated to the United States at this time. Time and again, he used the paper's influence and the funds from Our Sunday Visitor in support of these projects.

With presidential candidate Alfred E. (Al) Smith

A Hateful Campaign

The campaign against Alfred E. Smith, a Catholic and the Democratic nominee for President, was one of the nastiest, dirtiest exercises in anti-Catholic bigotry ever seen in the United States; Eleanor Roosevelt, head of one of Smith's campaign organizations, said she never knew what bigotry *was* until that campaign. Throughout Smith's campaign in 1928, Fr. Noll steered the editorial policy of his paper in a patient, charitable manner, without supporting one candidate over the other. He did, however, examine all charges being hurled at the Church by its fanatical contemporaries.

Looking back years later, Fr. Noll said that he felt that the campaign did have the good result of bringing bigotry into the open. Also, since the South had traditionally been a Democrat stronghold, the reputable papers there had also leaped to counter the attacks, thereby providing more information about the church in the largely Protestant area. Ellery Sedgewick, editor of the *Atlantic Monthly*, wrote:

Let us be just. This church, quite alien to most of us, has taught us a lesson in manners and in morals. . . . The ventilation of this festering sore [religious bigotry] is for the best. To the Americanism preached by Ireland and Gibbons[11] is now [joined] the Americanism practiced by Smith. The Catholic church in America is in the civic sense an American church. . . . To the limbo where it belongs, Protestant bigotry must follow. The conduct of the (Catholic) Church, high above reproach in this bad crisis, will not be forgotten.

The National Shrine of the Immaculate Conception

During the early part of the century, Catholics had been enthusiastic about building a national shrine to Our Lady under her title of the Immaculate Conception.[12] With the advent of the

Noll with picture of the National Shrine

Great Depression and the Second World War, the project languished; then, in 1953, Bishop Noll joined with Archbishop Patrick O'Boyle to revive it once more. The bishop often wrote of this project in the pages of *Our Sunday Visitor* and enlisted the school children of his own diocese to collect their pennies for the shrine. Through these efforts, he was able to raise about seven million dollars. He used his influence with his fellow bishops to get them to pledge their support to secure the funds required for completion of the Great Upper Church. Catholics in every U.S. parish responded overwhelmingly to this national appeal, allowing construction to resume during the Marian Year of 1954. Sadly, this portion of the project was not dedicated until after Bishop Noll's death.

The Light of the World

In 1936, Mrs. Marjorie Russell of Topeka, Kansas, sent Fr. Noll a $1 bill with a note suggesting that OSV begin a drive to erect a huge statue of Christ as "Light of the World" in the nation's capital. Her dollar was to be considered the first donation.

She believed that, since Washington had statues of many famous people, one should be there to represent the greatest human Benefactor who had ever lived. The idea appealed to Fr. Noll, and he published the letter in the paper.

The idea obviously appealed to the readers as well; soon, donations for the project totaled over $150,000. Various ecclesiastics and laymen alike, when consulted, suggested the purchase price of suitable land might be too high, and that the statue would not be noticed unless it was surrounded by

Bishop Noll speaking at the dedication of the new statue "Christ the Light of the World" at the USCCB entrance

open land. Then, a better thought occurred to Bishop Noll. Knowing that the National Catholic Welfare Conference needed new headquarters, he suggested to their board that the donations he had collected be used to help defray the cost of the façade on the new headquarters building, as long as it was made to show off the statue.

This statue, "Christ the Light of the World," stands to this day in the front of the new USCCB building. Seventeen feet high, it was executed in bronze by the Austro-Hungarian sculptor Eugene Kormendi, a refugee and a professor in the art department of Notre Dame, and put in place in 1949. In its day, it not only represented the fight against atheistic Communism, but also stood as a reminder for our politicians that materialism and secularism were winning over the stated values on which America had originally been founded: "In God We Trust" and "One Nation, Under God," both mottos in which Bishop Noll firmly believed.

The N.O.D. L. and the Legion of Decency

As mentioned earlier, Bishop Noll was named to a team of four bishops responsible for starting the National Organization for Decency in Literature (N.O.D.L.) in 1933 and began his own diocesan drive against lewd magazines in 1937, convinced that the magazines would destroy the morals of youth. Thereafter, the bishops took up the drive nationally, and named Bishop Noll chairman. He was also a board of the Legion of Decency, and when the League began to classify motion pictures, indicating which were morally offensive, the movie moguls began to cry "censorship!"

"Nonsense," snorted Noll. "Each viewer is allowed to make up his own mind as to what he wishes to watch."

CHAPTER TEN

THE DIOCESE OF FORT WAYNE

In spite of all his outside activities, Bishop Noll never neglected his own growing diocese. He set to work encouraging, building, and consolidating Catholic high schools, feeling strongly that, in spite of the cost, Catholic high schools were needed to protect young Catholics at a critical phase of their lives.

Here, too, his ideas were ahead of the times. Traditionally, religious orders ran schools that were segregated according to sex. Thus, Fort Wayne had a boys' Catholic school near a public high school, and both of the Catholic girls' schools were near other non-Catholic schools. But the Bishop thought keeping the Catholic girls and boys apart from each other — and near non-

Noll with campers at the Boy Scout camp in Rome City, Indiana; August 22, 1936

Catholics — was silly, so he established a co-educational high school. Today, co-educational schools are the norm, but in Bishop Noll's time, they were a novel idea.

Bishop Noll not only built schools but, knowing that many students could not attend because of the tuition, he set up funds to provide scholarships and established simple "work programs" that students could do and still keep up their grades. For example, when young Norma Macy began high school at Central Catholic, the tuition of $20 was still too high for her mother to afford. Instead, Norma worked to pay her tuition by keeping Fr. Lawrence Gollner's classroom dusted and helping him correct papers.

Because Catholic education was so dear to his heart, Bishop Noll took an active part in the ceremonies at Central Catholic High School and the other schools in the diocese as often as possible. At the first glance of the campus visitor, the students would pass the word, "Here comes the Bish!" Bishop Noll not only encouraged the students as a group, but as individuals as well.

In June 1948, Bishop Noll was handing out the diplomas at Central Catholic's graduation ceremonies. As senior Otto Bonahoom received his diploma, he was surprised when he also received a book. Titled *RESTORING ALL THINGS — A Guide to Catholic Action*, the book was inscribed:

Dear Otto,

Recalling your splendid Catholic Action work as a High School student, I pray you will continue it. This book may help. God bless you.

John Francis Noll, Bishop

During his high school years, Otto had appeared on a weekly radio program on station WGL called *The High Angle*, where

Inscription in gift book presented to Otto Bonahoom

high school students discussed a range of topics such as religion, morality, dating, etc. He was also the MC of a program on radio station WOWO called the *Junior Jamboree,* an ecumenical program that featured students from all over Northern Indiana. Although Otto had seen Archbishop Noll many times, they had never met, and Otto hadn't the slightest clue that his work had been noticed.

A few years later, while finishing his degree at Marquette University Law School, Otto found himself in financial difficulties without enough money to pay his tuition. When Fr. Fred Westendorf, his former pastor and his mentor, heard of Otto's difficulty, he made an appointment for the college student with Archbishop Noll. Later, Otto recalled:

> I vividly remember walking into the Bishop's stately office on Washington Street. He was cordial and asked me about my studies and my college experience and how much money I needed. When I told him, he pulled out his checkbook and wrote me a personal check for $200, the total amount needed for one semester's tuition at

Marquette. As he handed it to me he said, "I certainly want you to finish your education. Keep up the good work, Otto, and God bless you."

Always concerned that his diocese should receive the best in Catholic information, Bishop Noll arranged for the Catholic Evidence Guild to begin a series of Sunday night lectures held in the high school gym. A number of famous Catholics spoke, including the Trapp Family Singers and Frank Sheed and Mazie Ward of the Sheed and Ward Publishing Company.

Bishop Noll also implemented and oversaw a massive building program of churches, hospitals, a seminary, and an orphanage. Often, the projects were aided by funds from Our Sunday Visitor. By the end of his life, Bishop Noll had established 25 new parishes in his diocese.

Hearing that a lovely old hotel at Lake Wawasee, near Syracuse, Indiana, was for sale, Bishop Noll determined to purchase it for a seminary to be run by the Crosier fathers. He did so in 1947, using Our Sunday Visitor funds to buy and refurbish it. Bishop Noll named it Our Lady of the Lake seminary and added a beautiful chapel. He asked Elizabeth Kormendi, the wife of the sculptor of the "Christ the Light of the World" statue, to paint the Stations of the Cross there. Her large oil paintings formed a mural 150 feet long, and over five feet tall, that flowed around the perimeter of the chapel in a stunning panorama. At the twelfth station, a somewhat portly St. John was portrayed — with the features and red hair of the genial Bishop who had commissioned her work!

Bishop Noll built new diocesan offices and the Memorial Chapel in the heart of the Fort Wayne financial district. Also, he added Indiana limestone to the face of the cathedral so that it would gleam in the sun and attract attention as a beacon for people to see.

During the Depression, the Diocese of Fort Wayne was hard hit. As Bishop, Noll was well aware of the problems of many of the

Archbishop Noll painted as St. John in Elizabeth Kormendi's mural

parishes that fell ever deeper into debt, due to interests on their loans. Several parish properties were in danger of foreclosure. Although the Bishop of a diocese has no actual responsibility for any parish's debt, Archbishop Noll determined that no creditor of any parish in his diocese would lose a single penny of their principal. To this end, he personally spoke with banks and other financial institutions holding the largest notes of these loans and, pledging his surety, negotiated a reduction in interest rates to an average of 3%. He also wrote 1,200 letters to other creditors of the parishes.

Priests then, as now, did not receive much financial training in the seminary. Bishop Noll sought out someone skilled in finance to help in this grave monetary crisis and, in 1933, hired Ed Disser as a financial officer for the diocese. Disser was a banker who, like so many bankers at this time, had lost everything in the crash. In addition to being unemployed, Ed was the father of nine children. For the Dissers, this new job seemed like the answer to a prayer, and in fact they had just finished a novena to St. Jude, patron of the impossible, to find work for the breadwinner of the family. Bishop Noll not only became the employer of the father, but a close friend of the entire Disser family. (Five years later, when Ed died unexpectedly, Bishop Noll made certain that the family's mortgage was paid until the oldest son came home from college and went to work to help the family make ends meet.)

Bishop Noll then had recourse to Our Sunday Visitor, which was building up a fund for the support of the Missionary Catechists. With the help and advice of Ed Disser, he used these funds to establish the General Refunding Corporation and brought the loans up to date. In some cases, the loans were refinanced with the aid of this Corporation. In those days, no diocese had a diocesan fund, but soon, Disser and Noll's idea in establishing the Refunding Corporation was adapted by other dioceses throughout the United States. By the 1940s, the parish debts of over $7 million had been reduced to less than half a million dollars and, once people were able to return to work, the parishes began to be able to carry their own debt payments again.

Through the years, Bishop Noll confirmed 133,000 people and ordained 500 priests, many of them from the Congregation of Holy Cross at Notre Dame, along with those from his own diocese. He had a particular fondness for the Sacrament of Confirmation and always enjoyed attending to these himself, even when he was finally given an auxiliary in 1950. What to another man might have been only a time-consuming, routine chore was a

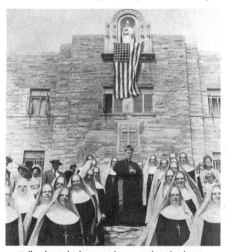

Noll welcomed religious orders to work in the diocese

delight for Bishop Noll. He often said that he found his greatest relaxation from his office and editorial work in visiting the parishes.

One reason he enjoyed parish visitations was his great love for children. Their freshness and innocence were a joy to him, and their often unguarded or surprising remarks were a constant source of amusement. One of his favorite stories concerned his questioning a confirmation class. Bishop Noll proposed the question, "What type of work did the apostles do?"

Immediately, one little girl waved her hand and practically bounced in her seat in her eagerness to answer. When he called on her, she responded authoritatively, "They worked for the WPA (Work Project Administration)!"[13]

In spite of his best efforts to retain his solemnity, the good Bishop wound up in a paroxysm of coughing to cover his laughter.

Bishop Noll maintained a lifelong dedication to evangelization, and as Bishop he often conducted Sunday evening information sessions about the Catholic faith at the cathedral.

A man of prayer, Bishop Noll was a fervent member of the Priests' Eucharistic League. This organization was founded by St. Peter Julian Eymard in 1858 and brought to Indiana by Fintan Mundwiler, abbot of the Benedictine monastery of St. Meinrad, Indiana. Devoted to the Eucharist, Fr. Noll established the Blessed Sacrament chapel at the cathedral, which was the first in the diocese to have perpetual adoration.

The Peruvian Sacred Hearts priest Fr. Mateo Crawley-Boevey toured the United States for four years, from 1940 to 1944, promoting the Enthronement of the Sacred Heart of Jesus. He believed that God's reign of love should begin in the family, from where it would reach out to all of society. His fiery conferences to clergy and laity alike brought fruitful results. Bishop Noll's friend Cardinal Stritch consecrated his Chicago diocese to the Sacred Heart in 1943. Bishop Noll, too, loved the devotion

Original enthronement ceremony at Our Sunday Visitor pressroom

The image of the Sacred Heart enthroned
by Noll remains at
Our Sunday Visitor today

and spread it through his diocese. He, himself, performed the enthronement ceremony in the homes of his relatives, and enthroned the Sacred Heart in the pressroom of *Our Sunday Visitor*.

In 1943, at his instigation, Victory Noll became the secretariat for the devotion for the state of Indiana.

How could a single man possibly do all the things Bishop Noll did? In addition to his own prodigious energy, Noll had a special talent for organization, and for recognizing others with ability. Unlike many who fail because they attempt to do everything themselves, Fr. Noll was great at delegating authority to others. One priest remarked that the Bishop felt that his priests could do anything, simply because they were priests. In addition to their parish duties, they were routinely assigned six or seven other tasks. With an efficient and organized diocese and a back-breaking personal schedule, Fr. Noll went about seeing what needed to be done and doing it.

"The Bish" at Home on the Island

Although he had a warm and engaging personality in public, in many ways Noll was a very private man. A man of simple tastes, nowhere was he more relaxed than around the members of his large and loving family.

After he was elevated to the bishopric, Fr. Noll always spent the month of July at his summer home on Bishop's Island. Although it was known as the "cottage in Rome City," it was actually a large, comfortable home on Lake Sylvan that had been purchased by Bishop Alerding and enlarged by Noll.

Bishop Noll's sister also owned a summer home on a nearby island, and members of the large Noll clan often enjoyed pleasant summer days boating from one island to the other to visit.

Even here, the Bishop's work was not neglected. He would spend mornings, after Mass, working at his desk: going through piles of correspondence, writing articles, dictating to his niece,

The "cottage" on Bishop's Island

Time to relax on Bishop's Island

Cecilia, who served as his secretary, and tending to the diocesan business of the day. Each Wednesday, the chancellor came over from Fort Wayne to go over the week's events.

Often, some of the priests and seminarians of the diocese

would be invited out for a visit. If they needed to discuss anything with the Bishop during July, they would have to go out to the island, since there was no phone in the cottage. (Some suspected he failed to get a phone in order to preserve the peace and quiet of his lake retreat.)

Naturally, when one of the priests came out, they would chat a while before getting down to the visitor's request. They all soon learned to make sure the subject of

Best mode of inter-island travel

Communism was not brought up. Bishop Noll was such a foe of this ideology that he would literally talk for hours about it.

Each day, relatives and friends from the other islands would come over and Bishop Noll would celebrate Mass on a corner of the large front porch. At first, his grandnephew Jack Fink served as altar boy. Later, another grandnephew, Steve Sullivan, gained that honor. Bishop Noll had a deep love for the Blessed Virgin Mary, and the boys were impressed that he recited the Litany of Loreto from memory as he unvested after Mass each morning.

Bishop Noll's sister Pinkie also had a home on Bishop's Island, down at the tip of the island and hidden from view of the bishop's house. Pinkie, who had been Noll's secretary while he was at St. Mary's in Huntington, often had guests at the lake, and they would all walk up a narrow path to attend the Bishop's Mass.

One Sunday, young Mark Weber got the honor of serving as altar boy. He was terrified that he might mess up on his Latin responses, but during the Mass all went well. By the time it ended, Mark realized that he was probably not the only boy the Bishop had kindly helped through the prayers.

Noll with his sister "Pinkie" (Muriel Noll Dougherty)

After Mass, Pinkie and her guests were invited in for a visit. In the den, a unique glass-topped table immediately caught Mark's eye. Under the glass were hundreds of wraparound labels from cigars. The Bishop loved cigars, and he had made the collection of labels.

Bishop Noll loved the children, and after lunch he'd often challenge one or more of them to a game of horseshoes. When asked if he would intentionally let them win, one of his cousins

"The Bish" with a group of children — many of them are his young relatives

Kissing the Bishop's ring as a sign of respect

laughingly remarked, "Certainly, but only if they were better than he was." He also played cards with the children and other guests. Again, when they won, it was strictly fair play.

Two families who were special friends of the Bishop also spent many happy days as guests on the island — the Foss Smiths and the Ed Dissers. Mrs. Smith had been a parishioner of Fr. Noll's in Huntington. When she fell in love with Foss Smith,[14] a Protestant, Bishop Noll gave him instructions in the Faith and married the couple. Smith later became one of the most active laymen in the diocese, along with Disser, the financial officer.

With his great love for children, Bishop Noll always enjoyed the visits of these families and made each of the children feel special. After they greeted him by kneeling and kissing his ring, he would lift each child up to sit on his lap and talk to them about their recent activities or ask them to read a page from one of their books to him. Later, he had their rapt attention, regaling them with stories of his travels.

As a special treat to the Dissers, Bishop Noll sometimes phoned and told Ed, "I won't be using the lake cottage this week. Why not take the family for a vacation there?" This free vacation for a family of eleven was a treat indeed.

Fishing for Men and Fish

Late afternoon and early evening were perfect times for fishing, and fishing was one of Bishop Noll's favorite pastimes. Out on the calm water, sitting still so as not to frighten off the fish, the fisher of men had time to reflect, pray, and think about solutions to the current day's needs.

One evening as he began to walk back to the house after a solitary and pleasant interlude, his young nephew Jack met him near the dock. The child's eyes widened at the sight of a very large fish on his uncle's string. Fr. Noll handed it to Jack and told him to take it up to his grandmother at the house. The boy took the proffered fish and began to run toward the house, calling out loudly in a childish singsong rhythm, "The Bish caught a fish! The Bish caught a fish!" The child's enthusiasm was so comical that the Bishop roared with laughter.

The Victory Noll sisters were often visitors at the island. They would visit for retreats, sometimes helping out as housekeepers. In early summer, the new postulants would go out for a week to clean up the house. This week would end with a three-day visit with the Bishop. Being new, they were not sure what to expect from such a great man. Invariably, they found him kind, generous, and loving and always ready to share a laugh, even when the joke was on him.

Once, finding a large shirt that was stained and full of holes, Sister Rita threw it on the bonfire with the other trash. When the Bishop arrived and began looking for his "favorite fishing shirt," Sister Rita's guilty demeanor and red face must have given the secret away, but the Bishop didn't pursue the matter.

Bishop Noll was such an avid fisherman that he wanted everyone to enjoy his hobby and tried to teach all of the sisters to fish. In attempting one of her first casts, Sister Marie caught a big fish — she caught the Bishop by the seat of his pants. Everyone found this so humorous that the two had to stage the accident a second time for a photograph, and Sister Martha Wordeman had

Sister Wordeman's drawing: Sister Marie hooks "the Bish"

to draw a cartoon version for the guest log (a book which all visitors to the island home signed, often writing little notes or drawing pictures).

One of the sisters was particularly squeamish and didn't want to pick up a worm from the can of the wriggling bait proffered by the Bishop. Seeing her discomfort, he baited the hook for her. She was terrified she might catch a fish, so she purposely wriggled her line until the bait fell off. Each time she pulled her hook up it was empty, and the Bishop would add another worm. Finally, he caught on and asked her if she was doing it on purpose. When she sheepishly admitted that she didn't want to catch a fish, he let her "off the hook."

Another time, as a group of the postulants was walking down to fish, Sister Rita was behind the Bishop, carrying the can of worms for bait. The Bishop stopped suddenly and the can of worms flew into the air, landing right on the Bishop's head. Terrified, the young postulant somehow controlled herself enough not to run away, but instead to begin picking the worms off the

The guest book on the island contained many clever drawings made by the Victory Noll postulants about their misadventures while learning to fish, along with their thanks for a happy time, and many little notes from other guests

Bishop as fast as she could. After a brief moment of silence, Bishop Noll began laughing harder than he had in quite a while. The shocked postulants — realizing they weren't about to be excommunicated! — joined in the laughter. Later, Sister Rita also managed to hook the Bishop, in the back of his shirt.

As Bishop Noll gave the sisters fishing instructions, he would intersperse pertinent hints on how to fish for souls. He lovingly gave them spiritual thoughts to spur them on in their quest for sanctity.

In the early 1950s, Bishop Noll received one of the first television sets in Indiana as a gift — even though there was no television reception in Fort Wayne at the time. When the Victory Noll sisters first came to visit after the advent of the new set, the Bishop wanted to show off the new marvel and turned it on for the sisters. All they could see was snow and the test pattern. But this didn't dampen the Bishop's spirits any.

"Isn't it a wonderful invention?" he said enthusiastically. "And just think, one day we'll have a station."

It was only after several minutes of staring at the screen that one of the sisters finally got up the nerve to ask if they could be excused.

Eventually, at the lake house, the Bishop could pick up a clear picture from a station in Michigan. Young Steve would boat over to pick up his Aunt Cecilia, and usually made it a point to arrive early. That way, he'd be certain the Bishop would invite him to stay and watch *Two Gun Playhouse* with him. Although Bishop Noll enjoyed the program, it was even more enjoyable when there was one or more of the children along. He spent as much time watching the rapt delight on their faces as he did the actors on the screen. Sometimes in the evening, Steve would return with his father and the three would enjoy watching the boxing matches.

Bishop Noll loved the West. He enjoyed listening to *The Lone Ranger* on the radio, and watched all the early western programs on television. He spent Sunday afternoons reading Zane Grey and other authors who wrote so compellingly about the American frontier.

Of course, all the sisters visiting the island were also invited to watch *The Lone Ranger* in the evening. Their strict bedtime was dispensed to allow them to view the program; then, they would recite the Rosary together before retiring for the night.

One evening, Bishop Noll went to have supper with his sister's family. Afterward, they all walked down to the dock together. As he started to step into the boat, however, he slipped, and the next thing his horrified family knew, he'd fallen into the lake.

But, unhurt, he came up laughing at the shock on their faces, and called out, "Uh-oh! The Bishy fell in the lake with the fishy!" At that, they all had to laugh as the portly Bishop, dripping wet, climbed into his boat for the trip home.

Bishop Noll was blessed with a happy temperament and a wonderful sense of humor. His young relatives remember him as always being jolly. Sometimes, he would tell them things with such a straight face that no one would know for sure if he was teasing or not.

Like any editor, Bishop Noll received his share of letters to the editor with complaints. He liked to tell that one lady had written to say she thought the quality of the paper had gone down. She wrote, "It wouldn't light the fire as well as it used to." With a huge grin, he assured his listeners that he had immediately answered her letter, telling her that he would make certain they changed the paper to include more sulfur.

A truly happy person, Bishop Noll recognized that a Christian was supposed to be joyful. In a little talk at the profession of some sisters at Victory Noll in 1936, he reminded them:

> The Catholic religion is a religion of joy. So many have the notion that religion takes away joy — that it is always reminding us not to do this and not to do that. The

Catholic Church always tries to hold out to the people
the fact that God wants us to rejoice! He sent angels from
Heaven to announce tidings of great joy . . . We want to
let people know that the Church expects the exterior to
reflect the inner joy. The sinner cannot be joyful. The life
of grace is the life which brings cheer to the person who
practices his religion.

Since the first of his priestly ministry, Bishop Noll had gained
the reputation as a peacemaker and was often sent as a troubleshooter when there was conflict, to soothe wounded feelings
or solve problems. This skill was not something new that he
gained at ordination; he'd made it a lifelong practice to work for
peace and harmony. Although he never ran from an argument,
most often — especially at home — his example and kind words
encouraged gentle settlements of conflicts.

Years after his death, a woman who had married into the large
Noll family shared a story about this with a good friend. She con-
fided that she was quite young when she married one of Fr. Noll's
nephews. She had been raised Protestant, and they were not married in the Church, and many of the other relatives seemed dis-
approving. When she was in the presence of Bishop Noll,
however, he was always very kind to her, never critical. Because
of his example, she eventually became Catholic, and the Bishop
blessed their marriage. The couple remained happily married until
death.

In all that he did, kindness was a hallmark of Bishop Noll's
actions. Two priests particularly remember his consideration
toward them when making parish assignments. Aware that both
of them had old, widowed mothers, he assigned them to parishes
near where their mothers lived.

Windows of the house on Washington Street

The Bishop in his office on Washington Street

At Home on Washington Street

Bishop Noll had planned on staying in Huntington and had moved his parents there. But when he was elevated to the epis-copacy, of course, that meant a move to Fort Wayne. The diocese had bought a large and lovely home on Washington Street for Bishop Alerding, which Fr. Noll moved into when he became Bishop. The 26-room stucco home was finished in Colonial Revival style. In 1935, on the tenth anniversary of his Episcopal ordination, a beautiful new wing was added which contained a chapel and offices for the Bishop, his secretary, and the receptionist.

When visitors would come and view the piles of periodicals and papers littering his office, Bishop Noll would caution them,

The altar in his private chapel

Noll's Chapel on Washington Street

The Bishop in his private chapel

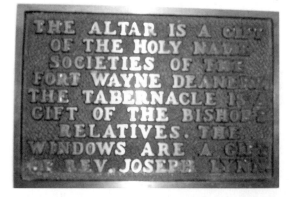

Bishop Noll's private chapel:

(top) Plaque in the chapel

(right) Beautiful stained glass windows adorn the Bishop's private chapel

(below) Tapestry over the chapel door

Mural in the dining room on Washington Street

"I want you to know there is order in this disorder!"

Bishop Noll said his daily private Mass in the chapel, a gift of the people of the diocese.

The stained glass windows were a gift from a fellow priest. The Holy Name societies gave the altar, and his relatives presented the tabernacle.

The house became a natural gathering place for his fellow priests.

On Sundays, Bishop Noll would often invite the Fort Wayne pastors for dinner. They would have a lively discussion over the meal, on all current business. There, too, he would talk with them about whom they wanted as their assistant pastors. This kept them happy, as they had a say in whom they would be living and working with. He encouraged all the priests to attend fraternal gatherings, sometimes hosting lively card parties with the usual after-dinner cigar.

With the family at Christmas

Bishop Noll and his brothers and
sisters on the occasion of his golden
jubilee of the priesthood in 1948

Pictures of the large and loving Noll clan

Bishop Noll with brothers, sisters, nieces, nephews, and other relatives at Victory Noll,
on the occasion of his Golden Jubilee of Ordination, June 1948

All his life, Noll had a particular love for children

At holidays, the Bishop would join the large family gatherings at his sister Loretto's home. There was plenty of food, and laughter rang out in the spirit of love as the little ones opened their presents after dinner. The Bishop himself played Santa, and always loved to see the joy of the children.

Bishop Noll loved gadgets and, on birthdays and at Christmas, friends presented him with all kinds of interesting and unusual novelties. A favorite was a music box from Germany, made in the shape of a little church. The children squealed with delight as, to a merry tune, a miniature image of the Christ child came out the door of the tiny chapel to give a blessing and a mechanical man on the side tipped his hat.

In those days, milk was delivered to the homes in a horse-drawn wagon. Dick Fehling was the local delivery boy whose route took in the home on Washington. Often, the Bishop would see the fourteen-year-old hard at work and invite him to stop in for a while to have a glass of the cold milk, augmented with a few cookies that "just happened to be in the kitchen."

In 1938, young Vincent Gocke began service as the altar boy for the Bishop, a post he held for eight years until he entered the military, early in 1946. A fifth grader at St. Paul's, Vincent lived only a few blocks from the Bishop's home, and was thrilled when his pastor selected him for the honor of assisting Bishop Noll. Each morning at seven, Vincent would come in the side door and skip up to the chapel on the second floor. He quickly learned to light four candles for the Bishop's Mass instead of the usual two, and that there were three blessings at the end of the service, instead of only one.

Usually, two of the Bishop's sisters and sometimes his brother or a visitor would attend. After the short Mass, Vincent would slip quietly out the way he came in, through the side door, to make it to school in time. Sundays, though, were special. Vincent was always invited to eat breakfast in the large kitchen with the Bishop. As they broke their fast, they would chat about Vincent's schoolwork and parish activities. The Bishop would share news about visiting prelates and other events he thought the child might be interested in. And, of course, there was always Notre Dame and sports to talk about.

Bishop Noll was a great fan of Notre Dame sports, especially Fighting Irish football, and went to a game whenever he could. Fond of his young altar server, the Bishop would get Vincent a ticket to a Notre Dame football game each year. On that happy day, a lively little group would pile in the Bishop's car, with his brother Joe as driver, and head for South Bend. As soon as he arrived at Notre Dame, the word would go out: "Red's on campus!" The entire student body knew of their beloved Bishop's support for the school's teams.

As the Fighting Irish were for many other American Catholics, the school's winning team and charismatic coach seemed, to Fr. Noll, a triumph for Catholicism. Whenever possible, he would also attend out-of-town games. In 1930, he accompanied the team on a weeklong trip to California by train for the final game of the season against the University of Southern California. The Irish took the game, 27-0. After the game, there were triumphal stops at railroad stations across the country, ending in Chicago with a ticker-tape parade. Then, a crowd of 25,000 was on hand to greet their return to South Bend. Overwhelmed with pride, Bishop Noll enthusiastically wrote to Fr. Matthew Walsh, CSC, the president of Notre Dame, "I knew that the men would not spare themselves because it was their last game, that they were going to win another national championship for their alma mater, for Rockne, and for the glory of the Church."

Bishop Noll's passion for football sometimes annoyed Fr. Walsh and his successor, Fr. Charles O'Donnell. Noll and other members of the hierarchy constantly requested tickets to important games and asked for postseason games for charitable purposes. At this time, it would be unheard of for a member of a religious order to say "no" to a Bishop's request, so the Notre

Noll with his longtime friend Archbishop Cicognani, the Papal delegate to the United States

Dame administration often had to get tickets from the faculty to answer the requests from bishops for complimentary tickets. To settle the problem of requests for charitable games, the school eventually simply banned all postseason games.

In 1931, Notre Dame's coach, Knute Rockne, was killed in an airplane crash on the way to California. His body was brought home to

South Bend for burial from Sacred Heart. Just as he had received Rockne into the Church and confirmed him, only a few years previously, it was Bishop Noll who received the body at the church.

Everyone's Archbishop

In 1953, Pope Pius XII named John Noll Archbishop for his contributions to the Catholic press and the work of the Church in America. The elevation was a sign of Vatican esteem, since Noll's see was not an archdiocese.

"The Bish" with his sister Muriel and her husband, Clarence Dougherty, on a fishing trip in Palm Beach, Florida

Even after receiving this elevated title, Archbishop Noll remained a humble, loving man with a ready smile and hearty laugh. No one found him standoffish or cold. His was a warm and generous personality. Although his sense of humor was well known, he knew when to laugh and when to keep silent to avoid embarrassing someone.

One evening, Archbishop Noll had been invited to eat with his friends the Dissers. The family lived in a large old home with an attic. As the meal began, a little bat flew into the dining room. Just at that moment, one of the older Disser girls entered, carrying a bowl of peas. Seeing the bat, she shrieked and threw up her hands. The dish flew through the air and peas scattered everywhere. As Mrs. Disser went to fetch a broom to chase out the bat and the children scurried around picking up the scattered peas, Archbishop Noll's eyes twinkled, but he remained silent and simply continued eating. Much later, everyone had a good laugh about the unexpected guest at dinner.

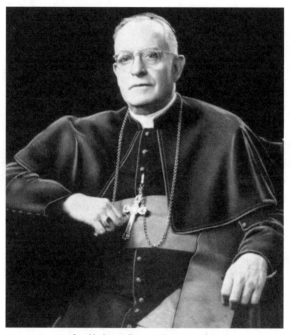

Portrait of Archbishop Noll sent to the priests of the diocese
in commemoration of his Golden Jubilee, 1948

CHAPTER ELEVEN

GOODBYE, GOOD FATHER

By 1951, time began to take its toll; Archbishop Noll suffered a heart attack, and was given the last rites at St. Joseph Hospital in Fort Wayne. As soon as he recovered, however, he went back to his normal full schedule of activity. As always, he retained his personal touch and continued to encourage children in their educational efforts.

In February of 1954, ten-year-old Janet Hester was the first winner announced in *The Journal-Gazette* National Spelling Bee contest for Fort Wayne. A fifth-grader at Cathedral Grade School, she was thrilled to receive a personal letter from Archbishop Noll which read:

Dear Janet,

Naturally I became very proud of you when I read in the paper two days ago that you had become the little girl champion speller in your own school, and I hasten to send you my best wishes that you may go far in the contest.

With a big blessing, I am Yours sincerely in Christ,

John F. Noll, Archbishop

He enclosed a lovely holy card of the Child Jesus and wrote a personal message on the back: "With Jesus, your Archbishop blesses you."

In August of 1954, Archbishop Noll had a stroke that left him unable to walk without assistance. In October of 1955, he cel-

ebrated Mass for the final time. Another attack in November confined him to his home. Unable to say Mass himself, he continued to attend Mass celebrated by one or another of his brother priests as often as possible, assisting and answering the prayers from memory.

In his final months, as Archbishop Noll became more and more incapacitated, his suffering became obvious, especially to those closest to him. He bore it all uncomplainingly.

Photo taken on the Archbishop's 81st birthday, January 21, 1956

One of the Victory Noll sisters had a lengthy illness, and was saddened to find that just when she thought she would be released, she would instead have to spend even more time in the hospital. Noll wrote to her:

> No one better than I can realize your disappointment at not being able to return to your community and the work that you love. I have learned that there is a great deal of merit in suffering a little bit. I spent seventy-five years free from sickness, and was kept busily occupied. Now, like yourself, I am able to do very little, and am expected to carry the burden in the name of and for Our Divine Lord. Let us pray for each other because we are both eager to get back to work, but must resign ourselves to the will of Him who loves us both far more than we realize. I said Mass yesterday almost blindly because my sight at

so close a range is still not good. I see quite well at a distance, but I cannot read a paper or a book.

Our Sunday Visitor's Contributions

Shortly before his death, Archbishop Noll sent a written report to the priests of his diocese, detailing the contributions Our Sunday Visitor had made in the way of financial support to the various institutions of the diocese. He confessed that when he was consecrated in 1925, there was not one single dollar in the diocesan treasury. The report clearly shows that over the thirty years of his episcopate, Our Sunday Visitor had pumped millions of dollars into diocesan programs. The amount was greater than the total of all the monies collected from parishes in that time period. In the report, he pointed out, "This story is being told to you not for my benefit, but in fairness to Our Sunday Visitor, which for a period of nearly forty years has been helping the Diocese of Fort Wayne without the priests or laity actually knowing it."

Although the contributions of his publishing company were made known in this report, most of the personal charities of this man of simple faith and generous heart are known only to their recipients.

The Archbishop's Final Days

The New Year rang in with vigor, even as the elderly Archbishop seemed to decline. The Alexian Brothers provided several male nurses who helped with Fr. Noll's care during these final days. One of them was especially devoted to his Guardian Angel. When this brother returned to his order and was replaced with another, Fr. Noll had a beautiful statue of the Guardian Angel sent to the order as a thank-you gift.

Unfortunately, the stroke left the Archbishop unable to speak clearly; only his beloved niece, Cecilia, seemed to understand him. She, who had been his devoted secretary and assistant for years, almost intuitively knew his thoughts, and his mind remained sharp. But, for a man who had spent his life in communications, the language disability was frustrating.

So it was that the Archbishop, who had once been so active, was forced into the inactivity of confinement. He accepted this as God's will and spent long hours in prayer, turning, as always, to his Blessed Mother. Brother Claude Brookshire, one of the male nurses who attended him in his final months, noted that his rosary rarely left his hands.

The evening of July 30, Archbishop Noll complained of a chill, so Cecilia fetched him some light covers. A young Crosier father, Rev. Robert Bliven, came and gave him Holy Communion, unaware that it would be the Bishop's Viaticum. Fr. Noll slept poorly, but was awake early. Around 8:40 A.M., he suffered another stroke, so Cecilia rushed to the phone and called Bishop Pursley, Msgr. Nadalay, and Dr. Raymond Berghoff. Nurse Case and Brother Hugo, who had been attending the Archbishop, were also there, along with two of the Victory Noll sisters, Sister Rose Elizabeth and Sister Mary Helen. Msgr. Nadalay anointed him while Bishop Pursley began to pray the Rosary. Although he did

not speak, Archbishop Noll seemed to follow along with his eyes until at last, about 9:30, a final stroke stilled his valiant heart.

One wag commented that Fr. Noll was a true journalist to the end: his death came soon enough to meet the deadline of the evening paper, and early in the week to meet the deadlines of the diocesan weeklies.

His funeral was a triumph

The solemn pontifical funeral Mass was offered on Monday, August 6, at the cathedral. Two of Archbishop Noll's oldest and closest friends assisted: Archbishop William O'Brien of the Extension Society celebrated the Mass, and Samuel Cardinal Stritch preached the homily. Two cardinals, more than 30 archbishops and bishops, and nearly 500 priests attended. Since the early estimates of the number of clergy to attend were so high,[15] a Solemn Requiem Mass, celebrated by Bishop Pursley, was held on Saturday, August 4, for the laity.

Ten thousand people filed slowly through the line at the funeral home before the Masses, and most attended the ceremonies, standing outside the church when all the seats were taken. Thousands followed in the long cortège after Monday's funeral, when the body was taken in procession to Huntington. Many considered Archbishop Noll a "national" bishop, representative of all the Catholics of America. For those of his diocese, however, he was their own: a simple man of strong faith, "home grown" and well beloved. They attended in droves to see him laid to rest in the little cemetery on the grounds of Victory Noll.

By his own request, Noll's remains rest on the grounds of his beloved Victory Noll

The "Lone Ranger"

It's probably no coincidence that Archbishop Noll's favorite program *was The Lone Ranger*. At the beginning of every radio program, a solemn voice intoned: *With his faithful Indian companion, Tonto, this daring, resourceful, masked rider of the plains, led the fight for law and order in the early western United States. Nowhere in the pages of history can one find a greater champion of justice.*

John Francis Noll — with his "faithful companion," Our Sunday Visitor — was a daring, resourceful priest who led the fight against ignorance and bigotry in the early western United States. Nowhere in the pages of history can one find a greater champion of the Catholic Church in America.

The simple marker on Noll's grave

Notes

[1] Fr. Charles Chiniquy was a Canadian priest who was suspended and then excommunicated. He became famous in 1885, when he published the book *Fifty Years in the Church of Rome*, which made numerous scandalous accusations against the Church. He spent the rest of his life giving speeches and writing books and pamphlets against the Catholic Church.

[2] A Protestant perversion of the words of institution, *Hoc est enim corpus meum . . .*

[3] The "interurban" was a series of rail cars designed to carry passengers from city to city in Northern Indiana.

[4] Later, Fr. Thomas Frederick Price joined with Fr. James Anthony Walsh to form the Catholic Foreign Mission Society of America, better known as Maryknoll. John Noll was among the first to help the fledgling group by establishing two seminary burses and advertising their work in the Parish Monthly and *Our Sunday Visitor.*

[5] This publication later was renamed and is being published outside Our Sunday Visitor as *The Family Digest.*

[6] Other publications of the same ilk sprang up in an effort to profit from the prevailing anti-Catholic sentiment, publications with patriotic-sounding titles such as *The Guardian, The Liberator,* and *The Sentinel of Liberty.*

[7] By the end of his journalistic career, Noll had written and published 50 pamphlets, with titles such as *The Catholic Church vs. the Federal Council of Churches of Christ, A Catechism on Birth Control,* and *The Parochial School. Why?* Although demand for pamphlet-style material has lagged at times, recent years have seen a revival in their popularity, and the company currently publishes several popular pamphlet series. Noll's book *Father Smith Instructs Jackson* also was used as the basis for Fr. Lester J. Fallon's early correspondence course of instructions, a boon to Catholics in remote areas and to the military.

[8] Early works published by OSV Books include:
Gems - David Battle - 1923
The Faith of Millions - John O'Brien - 1938

Thou art Peter - Josephine Van Dyke Brownson - 1938
I am the Vine - Josephine Van Dyke Brownson - 1939
Living Water - Josephine Van Dyke Brownson - 1939
Making the Catholic Church Easy to Know - John Walde -1940

⁹The Catholic Summer School of America, informally known as Chautaugua, was an eleven-week summer session consisting of lectures, courses, and entertainments. It was held in Cliff Haven, New York, from 1892 to 1940.

¹⁰ The United States Conference of Catholic Bishops (USCCB) is an assembly of the hierarchy of the United States and the U.S. Virgin Islands who jointly exercise certain pastoral functions on behalf of the Christian faithful of the United States. The purpose of the Conference is to promote the greater good that the Church offers humankind, especially through forms and programs of the apostolate fittingly adapted to the circumstances of time and place. This purpose is drawn from the universal law of the Church and applies to the Episcopal conferences, which are established all over the world for the same purpose. Organized as a corporation in the District of Columbia, its purposes under civil law are: "To unify, coordinate, encourage, promote, and carry on Catholic activities in the United States; to organize and conduct religious, charitable, and social welfare work at home and abroad; to aid in education; to care for immigrants; and generally to enter into and promote by education, publication, and direction the objects of its being."

¹¹ Archbishop John Ireland and Cardinal John Gibbons

¹² It was in 1847 that Pope Pius IX proclaimed Mary, under the title of the Immaculate Conception, as patroness of the United States. In the early 1900s, Bishop Thomas J. Shahan, fourth rector of The Catholic University of America, proposed building a national shrine in Washington to honor Mary. During an August 15, 1913, audience with Pope Pius X, Shahan received the Holy Father's enthusiastic support and also a personal contribution of $400. Shahan then returned home and persuaded the Board of Trustees of Catholic University to donate land at the southwest corner of the campus for the Shrine, and his passion for establishing a majestic "hymn in stone" soon became contagious to others, including Bishop Noll. As contributions and letters of support poured in from across the country, Bishop Shahan sought out the assistance of a Philadelphia priest, Fr. Bernard McKenna, to carry out the endeavor. Fr. McKenna was named the first director of the National

Shrine in 1915, bringing the dream of a national symbol of Catholic devotion to Mary a step closer to reality. James Cardinal Gibbons, Archbishop of Baltimore, blessed the foundation stone September 23, 1920, before over 10,000 faithful in Washington; Our Sunday Visitor donated the funds for the main altar of the shrine.

[13] In 1935, the Work Project Administration was formed through an executive order from President Franklin Delano Roosevelt. The project was designed to create jobs during the Great Depression.

[14] Foss Smith is likely the model for Jackson in Noll's book *Father Smith Instructs Jackson*.

[15] With today's jet airplanes available, this size gathering would be much easier to obtain; in the 1950s, however, most attendees traveled by car or train, which makes the numbers much more impressive.

Bibliography

Alerding, Rt. Rev. H. J. *The Diocese of Fort Wayne, 1857 — September 22 — 1907, A Book of Historical Reference, 1669-1907.* Fort Wayne, IN: The Archer Printing Co. 1907.

Burs, Robert E. *Being Catholic, Being American: The Notre Dame Story 1842-1934.* Notre Dame, IN: The Notre Dame Press, 1999.

Carey, Ann. *Archbishop John Francis Noll: Founder, Visionary, Defender of the Faith.* http://www.osvpublishing.com/mission/biography.asp, Dec. 2001.

Fink, F.A. "Life of John Francis Noll, Fifth Bishop of Ft. Wayne." Huntington, IN.: *Our Sunday Visitor* Newspaper. Series of articles, January 1948 to March 1949.

Fink, Jack. *Patriotic Leaders of the Church.* Huntington, IN: Our Sunday Visitor, 2005.

Ginder, Richard. *With Ink and Crozier.* Huntington, IN: Our Sunday Visitor, c. 1950.

Hull, Robert (R.R.H. on book) (Friends of Catholic Mexico). *Mexico's Persecution of the Church: Calles, the Persecutor.* Huntington, IN: Our Sunday Visitor, c. 1934.

Hutton, Rev. Leon M. "Bishop John Francis Noll: Catholic Action and the Formation of an American Catholic Identity." *Chicago Studies,* Spring 2001, Vol. 40:1.

Hutton, Rev. Leon M. "Catholicity and Civility: John Francis Noll and the Origins of Our Sunday Visitor." *U.S. Catholic Historian,* Summer 1997, Vol. 15, Number 3, pp. 1-22.

Larkin, Fr. Francis, SS.CC. *Enthronement of the Sacred Heart.* Pulaski, WI: Franciscan Publishers, 1970.

Noll, John Francis. *Defamers of the Church (Nineteenth Revised Edition).* Huntington, IN: Our Sunday Visitor, undated.

Stephens, Fr. Clifford. *John Francis Noll: A Centennial Appreciation.* Unpublished manuscript, Notre Dame archives.

Tucker, Todd. *Notre Dame vs. The Klan.* Chicago, IL: Loyola Press, 2004.

_____ "Archbishop Noll Mourned." Huntington, IN: *Our Sunday Visitor* Newspaper. August 5, 1956.

Other items:

Unpublished correspondence April 9, 1935: Noll to Rev. Michael Kenny, S.J. and memorandum re. Mexican question and National Catholic Youth Leadership Conference, c. 1934 or 1935, from files of *America* magazine, archived at Georgetown University Library, Washington, DC.

Unpublished videotapes made by *Today's Catholic*

Diocesan newspapers

And a thank-you for...

Correspondence and personal interviews with the following, among others. My greatest thanks to them for making this book possible. If I have inadvertently forgotten anyone, may Our Blessed Mother extend my thanks and a special blessing to them!

Bartsch, Sister Mary Frances

Bennett, Norma (Mary) J.; Fort Wayne, Indiana

Bill, Sister Alma

Bonahoom, Otto; Fort Wayne, Indiana

Buske, Mr. Don H.; Archivist, Historical Archives of the Chancery, Archdiocese of Cincinnati, Ohio

Chapin, Sheila

Crosier Fathers and Brothers

Disser, Sally

Eckert, Ann

Farley, Sister Carmela, OLVN

Fink, Jack

Flohr, Janet; Fort Wayne, Indiana

Geradot, Patty

Gocke, Vincent; Ballwin, Missouri

John, Fr. Richard T., O.S.C.

Hackbush, Janet; Archivist, Diocese of Fort Wayne-South Bend

Haines, Sister Monica, OLVN

Halbach, Sister Jean and the sisters of Victory Noll

Hickey, Tim; editor, *Today's Catholic*

Kramer, Sister Mary Ruth, OLVM; Coldwater, Oklahoma

Lahrman, Rosie; Cathedral Museum of Fort Wayne

Lester, Msgr. J. William; Fort Wayne Chancery

Little, Sharon; *Today's Catholic*

Lockwood, Robert P.; Diocese of Pittsburgh, Pennsylvania

McNally, Roxanne

Mensing, Leanne

Miller, Olive; Richland City, Wisconsin

Moeglein, Fr. Jim, O.S.C.

Noll, Hope

Noll, Kevin

Noll, Tom

Noll, Richard

Our Sunday Visitor staff members, especially Chris Meadows and Carol McCauley

Racne, Joyce

Rogers, Sister Mary Helen

Saxton, Amy

Schafbauk, Karen

Springer, Sally

St. Patrick's Catholic Church, Ligonier, Indiana

Stephens, Fr. Clifford

Sullivan, Steven

Sumpter, Sharon; Notre Dame Archives

Tucker, Todd; Valparaiso, Indiana

Vincent, Fr. John, O.S.C.

Weigand, Sally

Werling, Don; Director, Allen County/Fort Wayne Historical Society

Widmann, Fr. Phillip; Cathedral Museum of Fort Wayne

Wolfe, Sue; St. Patrick's Church

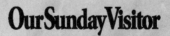

Index

◄○►